WORLD WAR I and the SACRAMENTO VALLEY

Special Collections of the Sacramento Public Library

The History Press

Published by The History Press
Charleston, SC
www.historypress.net

First published 2016

Manufactured in the United States

ISBN 978.1.46711.905.4

Library of Congress Control Number: 2015955757

Notice: The information in this book is true and complete to the best of our knowledge. It is offered without guarantee on the part of the author or The History Press. The author and The History Press disclaim all liability in connection with the use of this book.

For Amanda's husband, Brian

For James's wife, Lori

CONTENTS

PREFACE

The *New York Times* understands the art of photography better than most. This is particularly true with the paper's trademark "above-the-fold" front-page image, always able to convey poignancy that goes well beyond simple newsprint. One of the *Times*' finest images came out in late June 2014. It showed a busy Sarajevo street corner. In the foreground was a Volkswagen passing a gaggle of happy tourists with smartphones hoisted high, snapping photos of a huge banner picturing two men. One of them was a gaunt Serbian named Gavrilo Princip; the other was the plumpish Austrian archduke Franz Ferdinand. The former's assassination of the latter started the First World War. Written in English and placed between each man's image were the words "The Street Corner that Started the Twentieth Century"—a clever if not audacious metaphor. But was it really fair to boil an entire century of suffering down to a twenty- by twenty-foot chunk of Bosnian real estate? With further thought, it may not seem that unreasonable. The assassination was the seed of total war on a global scale—lost generations, a collective security scheme gone awry, the modern surveillance state, war agriculture, the rise of Imperial and Nazi German exceptionalism, the mandate system, the validation of women as the equal of men in war industry, the perpetuation of age-old colonial systems and so on and so on.

The goal of this book is to analyze the Sacramento Valley in the context of this epic event: the First World War. A vast majority of its content was mined from the Special Collections of the Sacramento Public Library. From original typewritten letters from the western front to published reminiscences of notable Sacramentans, it was pleasing to not have to travel more than a floor or two, at most, to find answers to our questions. Although these resources yielded a surprising number of compelling stories, few secondary sources covering the First World War were found in comparison to the Second World War, perhaps because the latter currently has a stronger grip on popular culture and also because of the sheer quantity of records borne out of the vast bureaucracy created in its execution.

In the chapters to follow, do note that the terms "Great War," "First World War" and "World War I" are used interchangeably in describing the same conflict. The reader is also encouraged to view each chapter as an individual essay covering a specific topic on the valley's Great War experience. As opposed to writing a chronologically contiguous narrative of events, the authors decided to identify the most salient topics of war—e.g. food, the draft, women, schools—and discuss them in the depth they deserved. A final consideration is the book's geographic coverage. Stories and mentions range from Shasta County in the north to Stanislaus County 280 miles to the south. However, because of the nature of the source material available to the writers, a majority of the work's content covers people and events within Sacramento City and County.

The First World War may not have been the "street corner" that kicked off the Sacramento region's twentieth century, but it is clear that bullets fired from a Browning revolver 6,500 miles away in Sarajevo eventually affected the Sacramento Valley in a profound way. America's entry into the Great War presaged several things, including the question of whether the conflict proved an ideal dress rehearsal for the Sacramento Valley's strong homefront performance during the next big war. At the same time, to what extent did it prime the nation and the Sacramento region to practice intolerance with so much more efficiency during the Second World War than in the First? As we sit within the four-year centennial of the Great War (2014–18), a consideration of the conflict has meaning that goes well beyond popular history's traditional fixation on machine guns and trench gas. The conflict offers a unique window into a community's—the Sacramento Valley community's—collective response to the extreme demands of civilization's first truly global conflict.

ACKNOWLEDGEMENTS

We gratefully acknowledge the contributions of the following individuals: First World War historians Terrance Finnegan and Jim Controvich, Sacramento Public Library director Rivkah Sass, central library manager Jessica Zaker, Carmichael library manager Roberta Boegel, central librarian Gerald Ward, library communications analyst Linda Beymer and library public information coordinator Tracie Popma.

We also appreciate the passionate and dedicated assistance of our library and archive colleagues in providing many of the images used in this book, in addition to those drawn from the Sacramento Public Library's own collection. They include Pat Johnson, Rebecca Crowther and Dylan McDonald of the Center for Sacramento History; Cara Randall of the California State Railroad Museum Library; and Kathleen Correia and Kelisha Skoglund of the California History Room of the California State Library.

Finally, and perhaps most importantly, we are grateful for the day-to-day contributions of our patrons. It is through their passion and curiosity that we are inspired to be the very best that we can be. Together, we are an irrepressible source for illumination.

INTRODUCTION

By Amanda G. DeWilde

On July 21, 1915, Colonel Theodore Roosevelt, former Rough Rider, ex-president and builder of the Panama Canal, visited the Panama-Pacific International Exposition in San Francisco to tour exhibits and deliver a two-hour oration on "Peace and War." Set on 635 acres overlooking the Bay, the fair was designed to celebrate completion of the Panama Canal and the rebuilding of San Francisco following the devastating 1906 earthquake and fire. Fairgoers were invited to look ahead to the coming years and America's growing opportunity. Hiram W. Johnson, California's governor and Roosevelt's 1912 presidential running mate, introduced the former president to a crowd of about seventy thousand at the Court of the Universe. The thrust of Roosevelt's speech, according to *Overland Monthly*, could be expressed in his life motto: "Be ready."[1] Roosevelt would not echo William Jennings Bryan's optimistic pro-peace speech delivered at the same site weeks before. Instead, he argued that while the canal was meant for peace, the nation had to be prepared for war, and Roosevelt concluded with an impassioned reading from Ezekiel 33:7, a favorite verse of his: "But if the watchman see the sword come, and blow not the trumpet, and the people be not warned; if the sword come and take any person from among them, he is taken away in his iniquity."

Roosevelt was fêted by the California State Commission during his visit and toured the fairgrounds extensively. On his second day in the city, he visited the California Building at the end of Administration Avenue on the Marina, where he reviewed the thirty-thousand-square-foot Sacramento

The entrance to the Sacramento Valley's expansive display at the 1915 Panama-Pacific International Exhibition. *Sacramento Public Library.*

Valley display. Upon studying the vast agricultural and mineral might of the region, he is said to have exclaimed his customary "Bully!" several times and delighted the exhibit hosts by stating, "It is one of the most telling exhibitions I ever saw. It shows the marvelous fertility of the Sacramento Valley, its agricultural riches and the industry of its inhabitants."[2]

The space did indeed communicate the Sacramento Valley's wealth and ambitions, all of which would be touched by the war in the coming years. The Sacramento Valley was one of several California regions represented in the 120,000-square-foot California Building, and the region encompassed sixteen counties in the Sacramento Valley and Sierra Foothills. Floor space composed one-quarter of the building at a steep cost of $75,000. Display themes fell mostly under agricultural activities: the farming, cultivation, canning and distribution of food.

On display were dried fruit mountains, a processed food monument, pickled and canned items, leather, hops, beans, nuts, raisins, honey, cereals and mill stuffs; three hundred mounted birds and animals, an ostrich farm and wild game exhibits; an operating model rice mill;

hydroelectric power and mining models; and a massive transportation map near the lecture hall where John C. Ing of Sacramento spoke daily. An impressive twenty-five- by forty-four-foot replica of the State Capitol housed the information bureau and restrooms. The exhibit's art gallery was modest but well appointed because J.A. Filcher, head of the exhibition commission, noted that "while our people are largely commercial, we are not lacking in those works that appeal to the finer sensibilities." Filcher, a former Sacramento city commissioner, resigned his post to head the Sacramento Valley Expositions Commission. He declared that the valley exhibit was the "biggest ever undertaken for the enlightenment of the world regarding the true characteristics and advantages of this part of the state."[3]

The war in Europe was ever present in the minds of fairgoers, who had been primed to view exhibits in light of the coming storm by orations from politicians like Roosevelt and William Jennings Bryan. Over the course of ten months, 18,876,438 people visited the fair, but they were there primarily for distraction rather than inspiration, and Filcher found that at the Sacramento exhibit, visitors voiced the feeling that "when conditions changed they might come out here to live."[4]

The Panama-Pacific International Exposition concluded a little more than a year after the start of the world war in Europe. Hostilities had been sparked by the assassination of the Astro-Hungarian archduke Franz Ferdinand in late July 1914. By early August, Russia, Germany, Britain, Belgium and France had entered the fray. For its part, up until then America had operated in relative isolation. Valuing independence and peace, the United States resisted formal involvement for nearly three years. But assisting the Allies while maintaining neutrality became more difficult over time. The sinking of American ships like the *Lusitania* and the interception of the Zimmerman letter to the German minister in Mexico heightened fears but did not move the nation to immediate action. Few local interests were considered at stake.[5]

Back in Sacramento, the quickly growing city was inviting settlers to exploit its newly reclaimed land. In 1917, the city claimed around 67,000 residents, a big increase from the turn of the century, when there were only 29,282. A few thousand county residents brought the total population to about 80,000. The region had branded itself as "The Heart of California"—not only a gateway but also a destination for home-seekers and investors. In Sacramento County, more than 100,000 acres had been developed by speculators and subdivided for settlement in 5-, 10- and 20-acre parcels for enterprising small farmers from eastern states. Colonies included Carmichael, Clay, Rio Linda and Wilton. D.W. Carmichael, mayor of Sacramento from 1917 to 1918, was a great colonization booster. He had founded Carmichael Company, through which he developed and sold thousands of acres of Sacramento land just years prior. He would also serve as head of the Sacramento Valley Association during the war years. At the state level, progressive governor Hiram Johnson, a Sacramento native, served through March 1917, at which time his lieutenant governor, William D. Stephens, took over after Johnson was elected to the U.S. Senate.

In addition to expanding into agricultural suburbs, Sacramento was pulling more neighborhoods into the fold. In 1911, the suburbs of Oak Park, East Sacramento and Highland Park were added to the area bounded by the rivers to the north and west, Y Street (now Broadway) to the south and Thirty-first Street (now Alhambra) to the west. The annexation tripled the city's geographic size and added thousands of new voters to the tax rolls. Suburbs were connected via a healthy system of streetcar lines running throughout downtown and midtown and extending to Oak Park (home to Sacramento's amusement park, Joyland), McKinley Park, East Sacramento and south to Curtis Park and down Riverside Boulevard.

Witnessing traffic downtown in the 1910s, one would get the sense that Sacramento had one foot in the twentieth century and another in the previous. Steamer passenger traffic reached its peak in 1913, with 212,000 people traveling between the San Francisco Bay and Sacramento aboard

Sacramento's bustling K Street is pictured on this 1917 postcard. *Sacramento Public Library.*

ships like the *Capital City* and *Fort Sutter*.[6] But the city also boasted 120 miles of paved streets on which pedestrians, bicycles, automobiles, electric trains and even horse-drawn buggies and wagons competed for right of way. The automobile, now a viable method of transportation for both sexes, was increasingly replacing horsepower on the road and farm. In 1916, Sacramento stenographer and YWCA member Alice Ramsey set the women's transcontinental speed record (eleven days), driving an Oldsmobile V-8 roadster along the Lincoln Highway from Oakland to New York City.[7]

The bulk of the working population was employed by city, county and state government; the Southern Pacific (SP) Railroad; and in agricultural work. Unemployment was at around 9 percent, according to a Bureau of Labor Statistics survey in 1915, lower than all other West Coast cities surveyed (including San Diego, San Francisco, Portland and Seattle).[8] Those employed in agriculture-related industry worked in farming, packing, transportation and the sale of the Sacramento Valley's bounty. The industry was substantial; the region brought in $125,000,000 in agricultural products in 1917. The Southern Pacific Shops, the maintenance facilities for the terminus of the transcontinental railroad, had the largest payroll of all SP facilities, employing about 3,500 men in 1915. Other major employers included the Western Pacific shops; Libby, McNeil & Libby cannery; Central California Cannery; the Capital Candy & Cracker Company; and the Phoenix Flour Mills.

Healthy banks allowed Sacramento to rank fourth in building permits issued in the United States in January 1917. Projections for 1918 included $6.25 million in construction, including Capitol extension buildings; the Weinstock, Lubin & Co. department store building; the Libby, McNeil & Libby cannery extension; and numerous other stores, apartments and warehouses.[9] Projects for 1917 included the Scottish Rite Temple, Hall of Justice, Native Sons Hall, Masonic Temple, Carnegie Library and Washington School. The projects indicate some of the community-mindedness of the citizens at the time. This was an era of joiners, and Sacramentans claimed affiliation with many local masonic groups, service clubs and religious organizations. Popular organizations included the Native Sons of the Golden West, the Elks Club, Tuesday Club and the Knights of Columbus. On Sunday, churchgoers attended Trinity Protestant Cathedral, First Baptist Church, Westminster Presbyterian Church and First Methodist Episcopal Church. Jewish congregants attended Temple B'nai Israel. Outside the city, the new Florin Japanese Methodist Church, inaugurated in 1915, demonstrated the diversity of the county. The Japanese living in the Sacramento River Delta represented one of the fasting-growing minorities in the county. Sacramento's foreign-born population sat at around 15 percent, with large numbers hailing from Italy, Germany, Portugal and Japan.

With so much change at home, how did Sacramentans respond to the war raging across the Atlantic? For one, the war was referred to as the "European war" by locals. Though President Wilson increased the nation's involvement leading up to the war, culminating in a policy of "armed neutrality" in early 1917, Sacramento was largely buffered from the conflict. Local clubs did host speakers from France and Belgium to share their suffering, and congregants at local churches prayed for a spirit of peace and mercy toward widows and orphans created by the calamity. Prices of goods increased as trade with European countries slowed to a trickle, and local clubs raised money for sufferers on both sides of the conflict. But it wasn't until the American declaration of war on Germany in April 1917 that the city was roused to action.

On April 2, 1917, Woodrow Wilson stated his case for war before Congress. Wilson declared armed neutrality "impracticable" and called on the body to formally declare war against the German government. He cited the uncivilized sinking of American ships by German U-boats and the resulting loss of American lives. If Congress voted to enter the fray, America would be fighting for democracy: "We shall fight for the things which we have always carried nearest our hearts—for democracy, for the right of those who submit to authority to have a voice in their own governments, for the rights and liberties of small nations, for a universal dominion of right by such a concert of free peoples as shall bring peace and safety to all nations and make the world itself at last free." Congress responded by declaring war on Germany on April 6, 1917, nearly three years after hostilities began.

A day after the declaration, the *Sacramento Bee* reported that letters and telegrams from Californians had begun pouring in the prior week, following Wilson's address, and the preponderance communicated "a large sentiment averse to war." Hiram Johnson, who had a stack on his desk a foot high, said, "I hesitated much to vote for the resolution and these protests were in my mind when I decided to disregard them and stand by the President." Representatives Everis A. Hayes of San Jose and Denver S. Church of Fresno were persuaded by their constituents and voted against the resolution.[10]

On the local level, there appeared to be more support. Sacramento's U.S. representative, Republican Charles F. Curry, voted in favor of the war resolution. His son, who worked as secretary under him before the war, would later enlist in the Aviation Section, Signal Enlisted Reserve Corps; be commissioned as a lieutenant; and serve overseas through 1919. Regardless of any ambivalence going into the vote, within days of the war declaration, Sacramento began asking how it would answer the call to help the Allies. Federal mandates soon reached state and local government and drove action quickly. Working through the State Council of Defense, numerous local committees labored to get everyone—men, women and children—doing their part on the homefront.

With few volunteering to take up arms (the state met only 22 percent of its quota), Sacramento drafted young men to join the fight. Most Sacramento boys went to Camp Lewis, Washington, with the balance off to Camp Kearny in San Diego County as members of the regular army or National Guard. Without the draft, which served as a lightning rod for doubt surrounding America's role in the war while also exposing fissures in the nation's social and political foundation, there would have been no army worth fighting the Central Powers.

Behind this effort, Sacramento farmers numbering in the thousands showed their support by increasing the production of needed staples and improving efficiency through mechanization and smarter farming. Housewives and restaurants also responded to the call of Herbert Hoover's Food Administration and pledged to conserve more and get creative with ingredients. Sacramento schools educated students and their families in patriotism and Americanization, directing their activities toward producing useful items for the war effort. And women mobilized as never before, serving through such organizations as the Red Cross, enlisting in the military for the first time and finding jobs in the local war industry. Every Sacramentan scrimped and saved to purchase Liberty Bonds, stamps and other war financing. Those who didn't rally behind the cause faced censure and even legal action. This sometimes extended to those perceived to sympathize with Germany or any Central Powers. The passage of the Espionage Act (1917) and Sedition Act (1918) gave teeth to efforts to silence the unpatriotic. Sacramento's story during the war years is highlighted in the following chapters, with discussion of the contributions of Sacramento's soldiers, women, schoolchildren and industry, along with an exploration of the attitudes toward unsupportive elements and recognition of the sacrifices of those who gave their lives in the Great War.

1

HOW THE LIBERTY BOYS SHOUTED

By James C. Scott

Just after midnight on September 6, 1917, the thirty-one men who made up Sacramento County's initial contingent of draftees stood cleanly shaved and modestly dressed in civilian clothing, all waiting to board a northbound train. Ranging in age from twenty-one to thirty and coming from settings both urban and rural, they were attorneys, journalists, switchmen, farmhands, chauffeurs and hotel managers. Had things simply stayed the same and the nation not entered the war, most would have been looking forward to the California State Fair, a mere ten days away. Instead, they were anxious, worsened by a one-hour delay and the evening heat and humidity that had averaged eighty-four degrees and 80 percent, respectively, for the month of September. When they finally boarded beneath the grandeur of the Southern Pacific Railroad's Victorian-style Arcade Station, not only was there relief but also a welcomed certainty that there was no turning back. "How those at the station cheered!" said the *Sacramento Bee*. "How the Liberty boys shouted, how the mothers and sisters and sweethearts waved their handkerchiefs as they turned their sobs into smiles as they realized that their loved ones were off to a war for world freedom."[11] Once out and over the I Street Bridge, the group would endure an eighteen-hour rail trip to the hurriedly constructed Camp Lewis, a seventy-thousand-acre military reservation resting on the southernmost shores of Washington State's misty Puget Sound. Just by sitting where they sat and doing what they were told, the thirty-one had consigned themselves to both the United States Army and the caprices of a war that was unlike any the world had ever known.

Five months earlier, and just days after Congress declared war on the Central Powers, a few thousand patriotic Sacramentans had packed Tenth and K's Empress Theater, a venue typically primed for the whimsy of vaudeville. On this day, however, they would hear a fiery Judge Charles McLaughlin exclaim, "It is time for men of affairs to lift their eyes from the dollar to the Flag. It is time for the mothers to consecrate their sons to the Nation. It is time for the youth of the land to forego all pleasures and stand behind the Flag."[12] Amid a sea of American flags and the din of martial music and applause, recruiting booths stood by for any young man interested in entering Uncle Sam's army, an army that stood woefully unprepared for a military undertaking on the scale that awaited.

As of 1917, the American military was well trained, even well regarded, but small, standing at 80,000 men, while an ill-trained National Guard, with its twenty-four training sessions per year, numbered some 127,000.[13] It was President Wilson's contention that, if war were to truly come, the merits and traditions of America's citizen soldier would emerge. He would call, and they would appear, for "if they did not," said the president, "it is not the America that you and I know…I am sorry for the skeptics who believe that the response would not be tremendous."[14]

Wilson was wrong, however, and as the calendar pushed into late April, only 32,108 men had volunteered for all services, well short of the 183,898 that had been anticipated. California mustered a moribund 21.6 percent of its quota, and despite a bevy of countywide recruiting rallies, Sacramento numbers were equally bleak. On the day of the declaration, army, navy and marine recruiters—located at both the Stoll Building at Fifth and K Streets and the Federal Building at Seventh and K—could entice but a mere 5, 12 and 4 enlistees, respectively.[15] Not sharing the optimism of its commander in chief, the War Department had drawn up conscription legislation as early as February 1917. The Selective Draft Act, after three weeks of legislative wrangling, was signed by President Wilson on May 18, 1917. Nearly overnight, 10 million men between the ages of twenty-one and thirty-one—an astonishing 10 percent of the nation's total population—would be registered and eligible to shoot and be shot at.

Fearing a reprise of the bloody 1863 riots that accompanied Civil War conscription, Wilson's secretary of war Newton D. Baker was intent on making "the day of registration a festival and patriotic occasion."[16] The newly formed Committee on Public Information (CPI), led by the talented George Creel, influenced state and municipal governments, not to mention chambers of commerce, to contrive a holiday atmosphere that would make registration near irresistible. By mid-May, California governor William Stephens had concurred by designating June 5 as Registration Day. It would be a day without excuses, a day on which public buildings would be made free for mustering and a day when businesses would close to free up young men from work, all ensuring that every American heart would beat in time to one unified goal. Sacramento anchor interests Lavenson's Shoes; Kimball-Upson Sporting Goods; Charles P. Nathan clothiers; Albert Elkus Menswear; Weinstock, Lubin and Company department store; and Breuner's furniture willingly conceded a day's profit by closing their doors. Next to the Southern Pacific Railroad Company and its complex of shops, both Weinstock's and Breuner's were easily the city's largest private employers. The Superior Court also ensured the closure of all saloons within the city and county of Sacramento.

Powered by locally appointed draft boards and scores of familiar faces with no connection to military authority, the draft would possess a distinctly civilian flavor. Secretary Baker's logic was simple: the act of civilians being registered and conscripted by civilians would prove more palatable than civilians being shanghaied into arms by federal officials. Again, this was a lesson learned from 1863's conscription campaign, which had been primarily managed by the army. Peter Shields, Superior Court judge and de facto father of the University Farm at Davis, stood as the chairman of Sacramento County's Council for Defense, which, drawing on the resources of the county's sheriff, recorder and assessor, was the local force behind June 5. The area's three Registration Boards were composed of 3 men each for a total of 9—5 politicians and 4 businessmen—while 170 civilian registrars manned the city's and county's ninety-six precincts, which came in all shapes and sizes, public and private. Folsom's Mormon Island schoolhouse, Galt's Shaw Lumberyard and the home of Ms. Nina Buell, known also as Buell's Shed on Upper Stockton Road, were three of Sacramento County's thirty-nine precincts. St. Joseph's Academy at Eighth and G, the Japanese Theater at Second and M and Harkness Grammar School at Tenth and P were notable precincts within the city's total of fifty-seven.

From 7:00 a.m. to just after 9:00 p.m., registrars plied their way through a strong turnout. With Shields viewing speed, accuracy and thoroughness as paramount, tallies and supplies were delivered by way of eighteen volunteers from the Capital City Motorcycle Club, who, zipping throughout the county at excessive speeds, found themselves immune from the "speed police" by affixing blue flags to the tails of their bikes. Illegal speeding in 1917 California was considered anything "in excess of thirty miles an hour."[17] Not even the governor could fetter the undertaking. When asking for a tally of registrants at a makeshift precinct located just outside his residence at Sixteenth and H Streets, registrar and retired grocer Henry May told Stephens, "No we cannot be interrupted, not even for the Governor of California," who then simply said, "That's all right…never let anyone interrupt you when you are busy."[18] In rural spots like Auburn, an effort to minimize distractions meant the cancellation of all dances and sporting events, while local forest rangers hiked their way into Placer County's more isolated pockets to ensure the registration of all those who were eligible.

When the count was complete, 6,457 signatures were recorded for the city of Sacramento, with another 2,612 drawn from county precincts. For a countywide population of eighty-seven thousand for 1917, 10 percent of all of those living in the Greater Sacramento area had registered with the Selective Service. If there were any doubt of the region's polyglot, multi-ethnic, multi-racial face, one simply needed to see registration rules, published and placed throughout the city in some fifteen different languages, including Chinese, Hindi, Hebrew and Russian, while Sacramento's three registration districts would hold forth men from nearly every race and twenty-nine different countries. Thirty-eight African Americans from across Sacramento County registered, not including twelve congregants of the St.

Andrews African Methodist Episcopal Church at Eighth and G, all of whom volunteered at the behest of Reverend T. Allen Harvey, himself a veteran of the Spanish-American War. Precincts within traditional Japanese and Chinese neighborhoods, the former along lower M Street, the latter along lower I Street, received a strong turnout as well.[19]

Still, various cross-pressures prevented registration from being a more rousing success, while at the same time casting doubt on Wilson's ability to find a popular mandate for war. First, nearly half of those who registered sought exemption. Physical or mental disability, dependent wives and children, marriage and ailing family members were the most common claims. Sacramento's own claim rate—52 percent—fell well in line with the rest of the country. By mid-August, however, marriage was struck as a sole criterion for exemption, making affidavits for dependency the primary determinant for release from service, ultimately meaning that half of all claims were rejected. At least one local newspaper, the *Sacramento Bee*, felt a duty to publish lists of those who made claims, along with the reasons why. The paper expressed, in no uncertain terms, that "in order to facilitate work that is being carried on by the exemption boards, it is the duty of every citizen who knows about misrepresentation, or attempt to evade military service…to notify the boards either by telephone or letter."[20]

The *Bee*—at the time Sacramento's largest circulating paper—had been reticent to support America entering the European war, but once in, the

Pictured in 1917, Yolo County draftees stand in front of Woodland's Courthouse. The county's draft quota called for 142 men. *Center for Sacramento History.*

owning McClatchy family proudly gave three of its own to Uncle Sam. H.J. and J.V. McClatchy volunteered for the California National Guard, and Carlos, who trained at the Presidio and then at Camp Lewis, went on to become a captain in the U.S. Army, eventually winning citations for gallantry during 1918's Battle of the Argonne Forest while serving with the 362nd Infantry Regiment of the 91st Infantry Division.

There were also scores of men who simply opted to not to show up, for either registration or the draft. Cowardice, political and religious conviction, ignorance, general disinterest and a desire to simply be left alone (particularly in the American South) were a few of the reasons they gave. One of the Sacramento region's higher-profile evasion cases involved twenty-one conscripts from Lodi who failed to appear for a Camp Lewis–bound train. The group's ringleader was Henry Mettler, son of a local vintner and member of California's American Patriots Association, an anti-draft group led by Daniel O'Connell. Both O'Connell and Mettler eventually were seized and jailed. O'Connell served five years in violation of the Espionage Act, and Mettler was imprisoned for "openly bragging that he would pay no attention to the draft."[21] There is also the compelling case of Irishman Michael McElligowt, a carpenter who lived at 222 Twenty-first Street in Sacramento. When asked why he did not appear for physical examination, he cited a refusal "to fight for any country that is an ally of an enemy."[22] That "enemy" was England, controller of Irish Home Rule and preventer of a united Ireland. It is not known if McElligowt went on to serve, but we do know that by 1922, he was back in Sacramento working as a carpenter. It is true that few of those who refused to fight went on to experience any significant prosecution. By mid-1919, only half of those who evaded had been prosecuted, with the government doing little more than publishing the names of evaders, as did the *Bee*, well into the early 1920s.[23]

Public sentiment could often be hostile toward those who chose evasion or stooped to claim exemption on questionable grounds. The term for one who did—"slacker"—floated freely about wartime popular culture and the press and was even invoked by public officials. The Godard J Street Theater's showing of the 1917 film *The Slacker* helped galvanize the word's place in Sacramento vernacular. It told the tale of a young man who marries to avoid the draft but is found out by his patriotic bride, who then teaches him a quick lesson in personal responsibility. Just over 308,000 Americans, the equivalent of twenty-five infantry divisions, chose evasion over service, a decision that was streamlined by the ease of it all. In an age without Social Security numbers and few drivers' licenses, outrunning the draft could be done with little complication. Men could slip out of town, move from spot to spot, change a name or two and lie low for the duration of the war. To counteract as much, so-called slacker raids—efforts to apprehend those who failed to register or muster—were conducted by the Justice Department, local law enforcement and groups like the American Protective League (APL), the latter a badge-toting army of citizen do-gooders.

The draft also radicalized a number of leftwing groups. Just prior to Registration Day in Sacramento, American flags were torn down from several precinct offices with anti-conscription literature posted around them. Members of the anti-draft and somewhat politically capable Socialist Party of California may have been to blame. By 1911, the party had won seats in the California Assembly and various mayoral offices around the state, the most notable claimed in Berkeley by J. Stitt Wilson. The antiwar Industrial Workers of the World (IWW), or "Wobblies," whose membership peaked at 150,000 in August 1917, is a far more believable culprit. It was thought that the IWW's so-called CCC Gang was responsible for the December 1917 dynamiting of the Governor's Mansion at Sixteenth and H Streets, which, despite damaging the building's foundation, caused no harm to Governor Stephens or his wife. Also worthy of mention is Judge McLaughlin's previously discussed Empress Theater recruiting rally, which was staged under the guard of city police due to a bomb threat that had been called in earlier that same day from Sacramento's Oak Park neighborhood. The region's registration drive pressed forward on June 5 with a mere four arrests in Sacramento County and zero reported for the rest of the Sacramento Valley.

The act of registration did not necessarily mean that one was going to be drafted. That determination came five weeks later, when the first of three wartime lotteries took place on July 20. At 10:00 a.m. in the Senate Office Building in Washington, D.C., a blindfolded Secretary Baker pulled the first number from a large glass bowl. It was 258. Remaining numbers were pulled throughout the day and into the early morning of the next day. Results were immediately sent to the nation's local boards, including the three that made up Sacramento County. District 1 covered all registrants east of Fifteenth Street, with mustering taking place at city hall at Ninth and I Streets. District 2 covered all those west of Fifteenth, with mustering to be at the California Fruit Building at Fourth and J Streets. The rest of Sacramento County fell into District 3. Local holders of the number 258 were Roy Clark Everett, a mechanic from District 1; Santos Trevino, a Pacific Gas and Electric laborer from District 2; and Orval John Fleischbein, a Mormon Island grocery clerk from District 3. In total, 721 draftees were tabbed, 310 from the western district and 197 from the eastern. Another 214 draftees were drawn from District 3.

By the beginning of August, selectees were called in for physical examinations. First to appear was Karl W. Oehler, a bank teller at the Fort Sutter National Bank and son of the German-born Reverend Charles F. Oehler, pastor of the German Evangelical Church at Seventeenth and L Streets. At 8:00 a.m. on August 4, the gangly five-foot-eleven, 133-pound Oehler made his way up city hall steps to stand before Dr. R.G. Pearson, kicking off a day during which physicians throughout the county would be examining nearly twenty-five men an hour. Falling some 8 pounds short of the required weight, Oehler failed his physical exam. He would not be the only one. Poor housing, challenging work conditions and questionable hygiene had an impact on the overall health of the nation's young men, leaving one-third of those who stepped up for examination unfit for service. In addition to malnutrition, the most common reasons for rejection included poor eyesight or hearing, poor dental health and weakness in the heart or lungs. Even so, as the nation neared full mobilization in late 1917 and early 1918, increased needs for manpower meant that summer rejects were well on their way to being winter inductees. Oehler was one such man to enter Uncle Sam's army under the modified standards.

Troop calls and subsequent camp departures were divided into four stages: the first in late August for 5 percent of the quota; the second in late September for 40 percent; the third in early October for 40 percent; and the last at the beginning of November for the remaining 15 percent. The area's first thirty-one men were ordered to report to the Sacramento County Courthouse at Seventh and I Streets to receive travel directives for a September 4 trip to Camp Lewis for training. Just prior to leaving, they were fêted with a buffet dinner at the Hotel Sacramento at Tenth and K Streets, where chamber of commerce official Charles E. Virden told the group: "Sacramento is well proud of you young men who leave tonight for the new army. You men, we all know, will carry the Flag on to victory and we wish you Godspeed."[24]

The next group—roughly 254 strong—left on the evening of September 22 amid the fanfare of a parade. Starting at city hall, the doughboys made their way east along I Street to Tenth, where they turned south and then west on K Street. It was there that each man was greeted by one of 300 girls from Sacramento High School, all gowned in white and pinning small flowers and American flags onto each doughboy's chest. The contingent then proceeded west, turning north on Second Street and marching directly to the Arcade

Karl Oehler pictured in 1918. After failing his first draft physical, the Sacramento bank teller eventually passed but never went to France. *California State Library.*

Station, all the time being cheered on by no fewer than 10,000 flag-waving Sacramentans. Just a few nights earlier, Oak Park's own conscripts had been treated to a farewell "smoker," complete with a jazz band, vaudeville acts and the standard line of patriotic speech-making at local barber Frank Cobarubia's home, located at 2908 Thirty-sixth Street. Subsequent groups were treated to sendoffs at Oak Park's Joyland amusement park, the state capitol grounds and the Travelers Hotel at Fifth and J Streets.

City and regional efforts to care for soldiers, sailors and their families were commendable. In the fall of 1917, the Sacramento Bar Association determined that during the war, and for a certain length of time thereafter, it would be "highly unethical, unprofessional and unpatriotic for any member to bring, maintain or prosecute an action against the soldiers."[25] The bar's commitment extended even to pro bono work relative to the crafting of exemption affidavits, provided that the reasons for exemption were honorable. It also set a moratorium on prosecuting debtors and those in foreclosure. In May 1918, the Sacramento Society for Medical Improvement voted to "care for, free of charge, dependents of those men in service who are unable to meet financial demands."[26] On May 31, 1917, the City of Sacramento made sure that any of its employees who had joined the military would have their positions protected. This gesture was supplemented in July 1934, when the city ensured that those service years would also count toward retirement pensions. Local businesses stepped forward as well. Dr. R.C. Anderson, a dentist at 1107 Eighth Street, provided a 20 percent discount for any recruit, making the cost of one's silver filling eighty cents as opposed to one dollar; Weinstock's offered free shipping to servicemen stationed either stateside or overseas; and the jingoist *Sacramento Star* (known for its one-cent price) rallied readers to contribute to an effort that would send hundreds of boxes of tobacco to Sacramento's doughboys.

It is perhaps through such gestures that we can see Sacramentans knowing a bit about the sort of war that their sons, fathers, brothers, beaus and husbands were heading into. Local newspapers, particularly the *Bee* and *Union*, pulled no punches in reporting Europe's butcher's bill. Articles contained startling detail of the new realities of modern war-making in places like the Somme, Verdun and Ypres: machine guns, chlorine, phosgene and mustard gases, high-explosive shells and fetid, rat-infested trenches. Often supplementing straight war news were occasional testimonials of local men who had been fighting in English, French or Canadian armies since 1914. The war that Sacramento doughboys were soon to join was on its way to destroying a generation of Europeans, a fact not lost on most capital-area residents, regardless of their support for it.

The typical Sacramento draftee was sent to Camp Lewis, an installation made up of conscripts from California and seven other western states that, in time, grew into the home of the Ninety-first Infantry Division, or "Pine Tree" Division. The camp's barracks stretched to three miles in length, while its 184 laundries washed away the grime that came with training in the soggy Pacific Northwest soil. Lewis's climatic opposite, occupying some 12,700 acres of arid mesa north of San Diego, was Camp Kearny, a spot whose initial charge was to prime all Sacramento Valley units of the National

Shown in 1917 is the enormity of Camp Lewis in Washington State. Barracks were 145 feet in length and could accommodate up to two hundred men. *Sacramento Public Library.*

Camp Kearny trainees line up to fire their Springfield Model 1903 rifles. In March 1918, troops received the more robust 1917 Enfield. *California State Library.*

Guard but eventually took on draftees near the end of October. Kearny's combination of California volunteers and conscripts, with an infusion of men from various other states, grew into the Fortieth Infantry Division, or "Sunshine" Division, named for the "memories of the training days at this camp, when they [*sic*] boys stood retreat under the beautifully colored sky of Southern California."[27]

For General John J. Pershing, leader of the American Expeditionary Force (AEF), infantry training was to take no more than six months: three stateside in the rudimentary forms of warfare and three in France with instruction in trench and open warfare under the guidance of experienced French and British officers. After inoculations for tetanus, smallpox and typhus, men were schooled—seven days a week; seven hours on weekdays and four on weekends—in using the army's two most basic weapons: the M1903 Springfield bolt-action rifle and the M1905 bayonet. At Kearny, doughboys aimed at silhouettes of German soldiers adorning the pointed Prussian battle helmet, or *Pickelhaube*, while also thrusting, butt-stroking and parrying their way to competence with the bayonet. Training then turned to two newer forms of war-making: gas and hand grenades. Each man was required to put on, and adequately adjust, his mask in less than seven seconds. John "Bing" Maloney, future superintendent of the Sacramento Recreation Department and namesake of South Sacramento's beloved golf course, was in charge of Kearny's gas-training regimen. Arthur Stark, who before the war had been a driver for Sacramento's Wells Fargo office, gave instruction in the use of hand grenades. Troops were then required to spend time in trenches "carrying on a series of attacks and defenses against the enemy."[28] No fires, no cigarettes and only whispers were allowed. During one exercise, Sacramento resident Sydney Haubtman, a former grocery clerk at Mebius and Drescher's, took things so seriously that he steadfastly rebuffed a captain for not having the correct password. Trench readiness would also involve hand-to-hand combat. A common exercise at Lewis involved the placement of fifty to one hundred men three feet apart with the task of defending a trench. Ten feet across from them were an equal number of men who were to attack the opposing trench once they were given a signal. With kicking and punching barred, a man was declared "dead" when he hit the ground. At the end of ten minutes, the side with the most men alive was called the winner.

The army's goal of placing a staggering 4,761 calories a day into each of its soldiers made for an impressive meal docket. On a single day at Kearny—a spot that varied in population between forty and fifty thousand—troops consumed, on average, twenty thousand pounds of fresh beef, twenty-six thousand pounds

Trainees at Camp Kearny engage in bayonet practice. The Americans trained for open warfare, intent on breaking the European stalemate. *California State Library.*

of bacon, five thousand pounds of tomatoes and twenty thousand pounds of potatoes. At Lewis, a common menu for the day included mush, hotcakes, syrup, butter, prunes and coffee for breakfast; macaroni and cheese, potatoes, catsup, pineapple pie and tea for lunch; and steak, baked potatoes, gravy, peas, celery, coffee and pudding for supper. Catholic soldiers were given special dispensation for eating meat on Fridays, the exception being Good Friday, and Camp Lewis's Jewish troops were issued traditional matzo flatbread for their observation of Passover.

With the Lewis and Kearny populations exceeding the tens of thousands, public health was a prime concern. Troops lived shoulder-to-shoulder, trained in dangerous conditions, were sexually adventurous and often brought maladies with them that hadn't surfaced during examination. Meningitis, mumps, measles, diphtheria, pneumonia and other communicable diseases were the biggest concerns. While Kearny's base hospital was massive, consisting of fifty wooden structures, the installation also offered three dental infirmaries, each with dozens of physicians engaged "with the work of fixing the teeth of the men of this division so they can bite the Kaiser hard once they get at him."[29] Some of the nation's finest physicians would also be streamed to camps as part of the Volunteer Medical Service Corps. By November 1917, the Sacramento Society for Medical Improvement had

Shown in 1917 is a practice trench at Camp Lewis. These were crucial in simulating European battle conditions. *Sacramento Public Library*.

provided twenty-four of its own for the service. Yet with the onset of the Spanish flu in early 1918, the sternest of tests for base medical staffs was still to come.

The army also sought to engender a certain level of spiritual health within its ranks. While building *esprit de corps* and making troops feel as if they were part of a righteous cause was a significant part of doing as much, Christian reform groups like the Young Men's Christian Association (YMCA) and Knights of Columbus (KC) were extremely active in helping the military supplant the age-old soldierly diversions of prostitution, gambling and drinking with cleaner forms of entertainment. These private entities, in concert with the government's Commission on Training Camp Activities (CTCA), toiled to encourage healthy living, instill standards of middle-class Christian behavior and promote more wholesome athletic pursuits like baseball, swimming and bowling. At Camp Lewis, YMCA representatives sought pledges from at least half of the men to read tracts of scripture that the organization was giving away, while nationwide, cantonments would sing—under the guidance of the ever-watchful YMCA and KC—a hymn just prior to closing each building for the night, regardless of "whether boxing, vaudeville, or a motion picture show preceded it."[30] Songs from early April 1918 included "Onward, Christian Soldiers," "Nearer My God to Thee" and "Faith of Our Fathers."

General Pershing was also adamant that his troops be protected from venereal disease. At Kearny, the YMCA conducted lectures on sexual hygiene or, as chastely stated, instructed soldiers "in the right way to live in order to preserve their bodies and minds."[31] While many camps established prostitution-free zones in the early going, it took Kearny until February 1918, when camp commander Major General Frederick Strong requested the closure of all dance halls in San Diego because of "women of bad repute."[32]

The War Camp Community Service (WCCS), in coordination with the CTCA, was tasked with organizing and overseeing an eclectic docket of good, clean entertainment options for troops. Actress Mary Pickford and Australian operatic soprano Nellie Melba visited the troops at Kearny in the spring of 1918. Baseball leagues were also commonplace, with Kearny boasting some of the best amateur players in the West. Live theater was popular as well. Kearny's "Volunteer Players" performed for audiences that consistently pushed capacity. Lewis constructed its own so-called Joy Zone, which contained concessions booths, two fifty-chair barbershops and a fifty-table pool hall.[33] Lewis was also a venue for boxing matches, including one in November 1917 that pitted the 364th Infantry Regiment, composed mostly of Southern Californians, against the 363rd, composed primarily of Northern Californians. Up against Charles Balerski of Van Nuys and past lightweight boxing champion of Southern California was Superior California's redheaded "scrapper" Private Goldner. Unfortunately for the 363rd, talent outshined industry, with Goldner going down in the first round with a straight right to the jaw. Troops' intellectual development also received a boost with the February 1918 dedication of Kearny's camp library, managed by Joseph H. Quire, a resident of Sacramento and former law librarian at the state library. Most books were donated by local chapters of the KC and YMCA, while Quire's support staff was made up of a cadre of volunteers from all around the state.

Knowing all that Lewis offered (and did not) was the Kansas-born, Sacramento-reared Hiram Paul Albert of 2617 Twenty-eighth Street. Possessing a knack for all things technical, it was prior to the war that Albert worked as a mechanic for the Universal Double Treat Tire Company at 1123 J Street. When it was time to register, he did so at Curtis Oak's Fifty-fifth Precinct, eventually going out with the third contingent of Sacramento District 1 draftees. Albert's prewar life was made up of fishing and camping throughout Northern California in spots like Hamburg, along the Klamath River, and Mutton Canyon, located just east of Georgetown. Camp Lewis's nearby American Lake offered him a similar outlet to nature and a way

Left: Hiram Albert at Camp Lewis. The Sacramento automobile mechanic would go on to fight in the Battle of the Argonne Forest. *Sacramento Public Library.*

Below: Sacramento's Hiram Albert enjoying a lighthearted moment with fellow trainees at American Lake near Camp Lewis. *Sacramento Public Library*.

to forge bonds with fellow recruits. By the time Albert was done at Lewis, his mechanical skillset had streamed him into the 91st Division's 347th Field Artillery Battalion, Battery C. His name will reappear at various points in this work.

Kearny's 40th Infantry Division made its way to France in August 1918. Once there, however, it was liquidated into replacement units for divisions already engaged along the front. Lewis's 91st, however, stayed intact. Of the first thirty-one doughboys we met at the beginning of this chapter, roughly two-thirds would go on to experience some level of combat while in France and Belgium, most as infantrymen with the 91st in either the 363rd or 364th Infantry Regiments. Other members of the first thirty-one would find themselves contributing as drivers, cooks and clerks. The 91st began to entrain for Europe in June 1918. After a six-day rail trip across the country, one that would eventually place them at New Jersey's Camp Merritt, the doughboys were refit with new uniforms, new helmets and hobnailed trench boots. On July 6, they boarded a series of ocean liners that would take twelve days to zigzag their way across the Atlantic, some landing at Liverpool and others at Glasgow and Southampton.

On July 23, after nearly one month of travel, the 91st finally set foot on French soil at the port town of Le Havre, effectively making the unit a full-fledged member of the AEF. The men were then moved to France's Haute Marne Region for training that consisted of drilling, long marching and maneuvers. Yet because of a severe need for frontline manpower, Pershing's desired three-month in-country training regimen would end up being more theory than practice with it shrinking to a mere month. By the end of August, the "green" 91st would be one of nine American divisions sitting at the southern base of the Argonne Forest and strung along an eighteen-mile-wide front between the Meuse River to the east and the Aisne River to the west. On the other side of no-man's land were the German army's crack 117th Division and First Prussian Guard.

For many of Sacramento's thirty-one Liberty Boys—over a year removed from that steamy September night back at Sacramento's Arcade Station—the time for going "over the top" had finally arrived. September 26, 1918, would be D-Day for the Meuse-Argonne Offensive. The AEF's six-hour-long, pre-operational barrage, powered by some 2,700 seventy-five-millimeter howitzers, was described as "so vast, so stunning, and the noise…so overwhelming that no one could grasp the whole."[34] Doing his part with the barrage, of course, was now Sergeant Hiram Albert of the 347th's Battery C.

Patrick Dillon was one of Sacramento's first draftees, leaving from the Southern Pacific's Arcade Station in September 1917. *California State Library.*

At 5:29 a.m., the Americans edged up to their fire steps and peered up and over the safety of the parapet. What they saw was a mixed pall of smoke and early morning fog, what they smelled was the sweet aroma of cordite and, seconds later, what they heard was a cacophony of whistles, sending thousands of the them out of their dusty cocoons and into the misty unknown. The lack of visibility would be an advantage to the Ninety-first and its sister divisions, but only for so long. With their advance, the doughboys were emboldened to find mostly swaths of barbed wire and empty trenches along the Germans' outer defenses but soon ran into the heart of enemy resistance at the "Hagen Stellung" and "Volker Stellung," both inner lines of defense that possessed higher ground, fortified trenches, barbed wire and interlocking fields of machine gun fire. By the second day of operations, the Ninety-first would be in for the fight of its short life.

Two of the thirty-one would fall at the Meuse-Argonne: Sergeant Ernest Wall, twenty-three, on the first morning of the attack, and Private Patrick Dillon, twenty-six, four days later. Dillon, born in the coastal village of Doonbeg, County Clare, Ireland, came to Sacramento when he was fifteen. It is there that he found work as a switchman for Sacramento's Southern Pacific Railway. The Indiana-born Wall worked as a driver for the G.W. Powell Parcel Delivery Company but prior to that was a member of the California National Guard and a participant in the Mexican Border War. Wall is interred at the Meuse-Argonne American Cemetery in Romagne, France. The whereabouts of Dillon's remains are not known.

Their passing offers a somber crescendo to what should be considered a very commendable effort by both the Sacramento Valley and the nation to bring the war to an end. Slackers, Wobblies, pacifists and the mobilization effort's general growing pangs aside, conscription was not only a successful venture in that it gave the AEF the men it needed, but it also proved a clear difference maker in bringing the Central Powers to a speedier surrender. Secretary Baker's careful retrospection, coupled with the CPI's public relations prowess, deserves credit in this regard. What should be troubling, however, is the huge gap between what history has long presented as a popular war and the veins of draft dissent found throughout the Sacramento Valley and the country as a whole. As historian Jeanette Keith rightly states, "If most Americans supported the war, as home front historians assume, then why the high rate of evasion?"[35] In an era that preceded the polling power of Gallup and Field, lacking no sound way of procuring a tidy percentage of those for and those against, it may come down to one thing: even if a large portion of the American people were against the war, they wouldn't dare say as much, for President Wilson and hundreds upon thousands of their neighbors were watching and listening.

In just over a year, Ernest Wall went from being a Sacramento deliveryman to fighting in the Battle of the Argonne Forest. *California State Library.*

2

FACTORY TO FIELD

By James C. Scott

America had been at war for well over a year when, just before 9:00 a.m. on July 4, 1918, a squadron from the newly established aviation school at Mather Field took off into an easterly blowing headwind. Once over Sacramento, the twenty-two planes split into two formations, with one descending on the city from the north and the other choosing to approach from the southeast. With thousands of stunned men, women and children watching from city parks, street corners and the tops of city buildings, each formation fragmented into an avian circus of loops, dives, spirals and treetop buzzes—or what Mather's flyboys called "flirting with the undertaker." Two planes then broke off, one speeding south to Stockton and the other streaking northwesterly toward Woodland and other points throughout Yolo County, all part of a promise made by base commander Lieutenant Colonel Del Emmons to provide as many valley residents as possible with an Independence Day thrill. Before their return to Mather, every plane descended to an elevation that was fit for dropping a friendly payload of Red Cross literature, army and navy recruiting posters and hundreds of silken American flags.

The aviators who took part in the Fourth of July spectacle, members of the newly formed U.S. Army Air Service, flew the most famous American-made aircraft of the Great War: the Curtiss JN-4 "Jenny." Sturdy and uncomplicated, the Jenny was considered special. Over its seven months of operation at Mather, it helped graduate eleven classes while logging some 29,939 hours of flight time and two million miles of distance. What made

Mather's JN-4s particularly special was that almost all of them were built just a stone's throw from the state capitol building at North Sacramento's Liberty Iron Works. Based along the southernmost end of a then dusty Del Paso Boulevard with a three-hundred-foot frontage on the American River, the factory had been a manufacturer of everything from electric motors to water-pumping machinery, operating under the name of Globe Iron Works. Spearheading its wartime conversion was an aggressive Sacramento Consolidated Chamber of Commerce, led by President Charles Virden and Secretary Henry Maddox. The chamber quickly embraced its role as a bringer of economic opportunity but tempered the Liberty and Mather hysteria. Maddox said that while both would "be of great benefit to Sacramento financially…it [had] a bad outside effect to measure such benefits solely from a monetary standpoint…putting the dollar ahead of patriotism."[36]

And the chamber certainly did its patriotic bit. Virden was the muscle behind Sacramento's record-breaking second and third Liberty Loan bond drives, and Maddox spent hundreds of non-chamber hours assisting in food administration. But to those who mattered, the duo had struck gold, and it was Mather, in particular, which stood out as *the* prize. Maddox declared it "the single biggest enterprise in which he ever had a hand" and one that would go on to change the economic and cultural destiny of the Sacramento Region.[37]

Having just started in 1907, America's entry into military aviation was a new thing. Yet with the world's first flight taking place in 1903, aviation as a transportation concept was not much older. Beyond the rare exhibition at the California State Fair, how many Sacramentans had actually seen an airplane before, let alone an airport? In the isolated valley town of Willows, located one hundred miles north of the Capital City, Mather pilots landed in open fields to the unbridled excitement of running children and speeding cars. It was the first time that many local residents had ever seen an airplane, known in 1917 parlance as an "aeroplane." One week earlier, nine of Mather's Jennies had flown over McKinley Park in a v-shaped formation that sent onlookers into a frenzy, with the local paper assuring readers that "no bombs were dropped, and beyond a few strained neck muscles no casualties resulted."[38] The city become so enthralled with Mather that, by late June 1918, an opaque fence had been constructed along the base's northern edge as a way to keep civilian "sightseers" at a distance and cadets focused on the huge task before them.

And they needed all the focus they could get. As of April 6, 1917—the day America declared war on the Central Powers—not one American air unit had been trained for combat. Moreover, the army had just 55 training planes, all of which were obsolete.[39] By the end of May, however, plans were in place for a massive 22,625-plane U.S. Air Corps, powered by seventy-five thousand pilots, mechanics and support staff, and a training program that would have 263 squadrons ready for combat and in Europe by the end of June 1918. While reality tells us that only half the proposed number of planes were produced, it is the ten thousand American pilots who were trained over the course of the war that tell us quite something else. Within a year, it would be a constellation of "ground schools"—which included the University of Texas–Austin, the University of California–Berkeley, the University of Illinois at Urbana-Champaign, Princeton, Cornell, Georgia Tech, the Massachusetts Institute of Technology, the Ohio State University and aviation training fields (twenty-seven stateside and sixteen in Europe)—that had done the job, training up a competent air corps.

With the chamber's Henry Maddox as their obliging host, War Department officials visited Sacramento in January 1918. In search of a suitable location for an aviation school, they looked at various sites, including one fourteen miles north of Sacramento in a spot called Pleasant Grove. However, one stretch of land near Mills Station, located twelve miles southeast of the capital, was judged to be superior based on "the prevalence of winds."[40] The area's mild weather conditions were conducive to year-round training, as verified by San Diego's North Island Naval Air Station, established in 1917, which was able to prepare aviators in half the time it took to do the same in the less-moderate climes of Texas and points farther east. In fact, by mid-September 1918, only three hours of flight time had been lost to weather conditions at Mather, and that mostly had to do with dust. Another factor favorable to Mills Station was its positioning just to the south of the Southern Pacific east–west mainline, which enabled the easy rail delivery of building materials, base supplies and, eventually, planes.

Not long after digging its way through weather records dating back to 1849 at the offices of the Sacramento branch of the U.S. Weather Service, the army made its decision on February 21, 1918—Mills Station would be the spot, and Sacramento was finally on the Great War map. By the end of February, 789 acres of land—previously the sleepy realm of wheat stands, cattle and rattlesnakes—were earmarked for clearance, and by late May, they were made "level as a billiards table," including the uprooting of 41 acres of primeval vineyards that had been planted by French émigré Joseph Routier prior to the Civil War. The entire acquisition was leased by the controlling Natomas Company to the federal government for a cost of $1 per year for

Mather Field is shown in 1918. Sprinkler lines are visible to the right. To the upper left is the SP spur. *Center for Sacramento History.*

five years, with the War Department able to purchase the land at any time for $100 an acre.

This opened the door to a sixty-day miracle, composed of a $35,000 modern sewage system; a $46,000, two-and-a-half-mile railroad spur off the SP mainline; fifty-two buildings; twelve hangars (each fit for housing six planes); two miles of macadamized roads; a 138-foot-high water tower; a 100-foot swim tank (paid for by the Sacramento Chamber of Commerce); and a baseball field. The $1 million school also would become the germ of 2,500 new Sacramento-area jobs, including a team of 1,200 contractors that was brought in daily on a twelve-car train.

Things were moving quickly. But along the way, Major Bascom Johnson, director of the Law Enforcement Division of the army's Sanitary Corps, demanded that the City and County of Sacramento tighten up their "moral status…with respect to prostitution and the sale of ardent spirits."[41] Emboldened by the efforts of late nineteenth-century Christian social reformers, Johnson, an ex-Olympian, health enthusiast and champion of the Woman's Christian Temperance Union, spoke for a new paradigm of decency in military training. "Taxi drivers who act like pimps, or go-betweens, or bellhops and others of like character must be weeded out," said Johnson. "Landladies of rooming houses…must conduct them in a proper manner."[42] As losing the school was the last thing the city commission wanted, it quickly complied with Johnson's wishes, voting unanimously on May 22 to remediate the most questionable parts of the city's West End. On June 21, county supervisors followed suit, voting to close all saloons situated within a five-mile radius of the school, including Jack Hinter's Saloon at Routier Station, the Moffat Saloon at Mayhew's Station, the Eagle's Nest on Jackson Road, the Arganda at Walsh's Station and John Studarus's Saloon at Mills Station.

The school also needed a formal name. By the spring of 1918, not a single air corps pilot had fired a shot in anger, but heroes were still easy to find. Carl S. Mather was a pioneer. As an aviation junky during a time when there were few, he built his own planes and flew in competitions throughout the Midwest, in proximity to his hometown of Paw Paw, Michigan. At age twenty-one, he worked for the Curtiss Aircraft Company, and at twenty-three, he volunteered for the new air corps. Mather was already an experienced pilot but was still required to complete his basic flight training at the University of Illinois at Urbana-Champaign, graduating in October 1917 and then completing flight school in January 1918 at Ellington Field, Texas. Five days after Mather received his commission as a second lieutenant, his JN-4 collided with another in a dense fog that had drifted inland from the Gulf of Mexico. Mather and one other pilot died. In his honor, classmates at Ellington requested that the new aviation school at Mills Station be named in his honor. By May 1918, the school was formally known as Mather Field.

In mid-June, Mather's inaugural class of forty-four cadets had arrived from the ground school at the University of California–Berkeley. It was there, over an eight-week stretch, that cadets had been trained in the basics of flight theory, radio operation, gunnery and flight mechanics. Although somewhat proudly roaming campus in their standard doughboy uniforms, the bleached white strip of cloth that ringed their campaign hats and a blue patch stitched to their arms would stand out as bothersome reminders of their cadet status. At the end of flight training, the strips and patches would be gone and the coveted Reserve Military Aviator's silver-colored "winged propeller" badge pinned to their chests. And yet, with months still to go, there was so much to know and not a single one of them had ever soloed.

As self-assured as the American military was, it did not go into flight training without consulting Great Britain, France and Italy on best practices, ultimately adopting a cross-section of each nation's training doctrines. Great Britain's Gosport method, one utilizing a rubber speaking tube that

Cadets of the University of California–Berkeley's ground school are shown in the spring of 1918. Their next stop would be Mather Field, Sacramento. *Center for Sacramento History.*

connected both trainer and trainee, was likely the most valuable tool that the Americans would adopt. The technique was aggressive, speedy and appealed to America's desire to meet its demanding timeline. With Gosport set into motion, Mather's training regimen was broken into five essential parts: 1) primary instruction with the instructor flying; 2) secondary instruction with the cadet flying; 3) soloing; 4) long-range soloing; and 5) academic instruction, taught by the aptly named "Kiwis"—instructors who did not fly. By the time a trainee won his silver wings, he had been required to log a minimum of sixty hours of flight time. To give some idea of Gosport's pace, most Mather cadets were soloing after just two hours of primary instruction. And with Gosport's functionality predicated on speed, mistakes could be made. Statistically speaking, for every sixty-five commissions earned, there would be one fatality. Over Mather's seven months of training operations, three cadets and two trainers were killed in flight accidents.

Flight training may have been Mather's primary charge, but it was far from the only one. Cadets also had to be trained to kill. They practiced

A gaggle of JN-4s sits along Mather's dusty flight line. Dust was a major problem, affecting visibility as well as engine performance. *Sacramento Public Library.*

aerial gunnery with American-made Lewis guns, which were fired from a trip cord positioned by the pilot's seat. Targets were either balloons or sandbags suspended by parachutes. Cadets were also required to fix purposely jammed weapons while in flight. Navigation was done with a simple map, note-taking and visual waypoints, and bombing was practiced by dropping sandbags over targets placed within a small reservoir near Sloughhouse. Base commander Emmons also made it clear that Mather's cadets were infantrymen first and aviators second, ensuring that they trained as riflemen for one hour a day.

Offering a window into Mather's training tenor was one of the school's first cadets, Maine-born Herbert Kennedy Morse. A few years before America's entry into the war, and while a student at Stanford University, Morse recalled being at a rugby match between Berkeley and Stanford when, just prior to the start, a plane flew over the stadium and dropped the game ball at midfield. From that point forward, he was hooked, and within weeks, Morse was enrolled at the Berkeley ground school. Once reaching Mather, he remembered the interior of his Jenny as sparse—an altimeter, tachometer, compass and no gauge for fuel, the consumption of which was tracked by math and estimation. Morse did run out of fuel one time, forcing him to land in a Dixon wheat field. As he puts it, "Sure enough I had several men bringing me five gallon cans of gasoline. Everyone from town came out, too, because they'd never seen a plane land at Dixon."[43]

The newness of the Jenny also meant that not all instructors were privy to all the plane's operations, leaving cadets, in this case Morse, to literally learn on the fly:

> *One time I was making a bad loop and the engine stalled. Well, I remember from starting a car that if you drive downhill the engine will revolve. So I dove steeply, the propeller started going around and then the engine started and I learned that on my own.*[44]

By the time Morse graduated with Mather's first class in September 1918 (only twenty-six of the original forty-four cadets did so), he had accrued some one hundred hours of flight time, well beyond the roughly sixty hours that were required. By receiving his silver wings, Morse was given the choice of staying on at Mather as an instructor or becoming a bomber or pursuit pilot. Given his patriotic sensibilities, he thought it would be nice "to fly to Germany and drop a bomb on the Kaiser."[45] But before he could get overseas, the Armistice was declared, and by 1920 he was back at Stanford.

One of Mather's most pervasive hobgoblins was dust. For the duration of the war, the school's flight line was composed of nothing more than dirt and grass, which presented a problem during Sacramento's long, dry summer months. Dust not only affected visibility, but it also created particulates that could affect the performance of the JN-4's Liberty engine. Initial efforts to quell dust plumes came in the form of either the mass planting of Bermuda and rye grass or sprinkling the flight line with water brought from the American River by animal-drawn wagons. By July, a huge step toward solving the dust problem had come about when two massive, motor-driven sprinklers were installed. An additional nuisance came in the form of squirrels and the hundreds of holes of their creation peppering the Mather flight line. In early September, a force of twenty-five privates made their way across parts of the installation sprinkling poisonous barley wherever they could, ultimately decimating, in the words of the *Bee*, "this squirrel reserve from the ranks of the enemy."[46]

Of the fauna that Mather could not have enough of, messenger pigeons were at the top of the list. As a certain base publication said, it was "in the little green loft a few yards north of the base headquarters" where one could find "humor, romance, and tragedy."[47] Lieutenant W.D. Parrott's eighty-one-member pigeon squad was essential to communication, delivering messages to observation posts, administrative offices in Sacramento proper and other spots around the county. Perhaps the school's most impressive service bird was Determination, which recorded a record-breaking flight time of six minutes, thirty seconds for the nine-mile trip from Mather to downtown Sacramento. Other members of the pigeon corps were Rusty, Sacramento Hobo, Speeder, Lena, Jack Johnson, Frogface, Baldface and Oil House Jimmy. All the birds were marked as government property by way of an aluminum leg case, which came in handy if pigeons were to wander off course. It was also in its leg case that a bird could carry up to fifteen feet in message film. Well trained, well conditioned and dedicated, the Great War's pigeons saved lives. This was most aptly illustrated by Cher Ami, the little savior of America's Lost Battalion during the Battle of the Argonne Forest in October 1918. Shot out of the sky by German riflemen, Cher Ami gathered herself and again took flight, blazing twenty-five miles in twenty-five minutes and ultimately halting a devastating hail of friendly fire with the following communiqué: "We are along the road parallel to 276.4. Our own artillery is dropping a barrage directly on us. For heaven's sake, stop it."

Alleviating the stresses of training for Mather's "man-birds" were several entertainment opportunities. Swimming in the nearby American River, making jam from the remnants of the old Routier vineyard and playing leapfrog or "Swat the Kaiser" under the wholesome influence of the YMCA and Catholic Knights were a few of the simpler pleasures at Mather. Akin to "Duck, Duck, Goose," "Swat the Kaiser" was played with one soldier, strap in hand, chasing another around a circle of twenty-five, attempting to hit the pursued before he could get back to his original spot. Amusement also came in the form of organized sport, equipment for which was funded by donations from the local Masons. Nicknamed the "Aces" or "Matherites," the school's baseball and football teams competed actively with regional schools, club teams and other military posts. The baseball Aces' least flattering moment came in August 1918 with a defeat at the hands of the prison team from Represa, 8–0. Football was a different story; led by University of Pittsburgh All-American and future Pittsburgh Pirate Jimmy De Hart, the Aces defeated the likes of the Presidio, Fort Baker, UC-Berkeley, St. Mary's College and Stanford. Boxing was all the rage, along with intramural leagues for basketball, baseball and football. Cadets could also go to Sacramento when granted liberty. Riding into the city was commonly done by train or by simply hailing down one of the many civilians, who were more than willing to transport a flyboy just to be able to proudly tell any and all that they had done so.

Mather also had room for more intellectual pursuits. French classes were common, as were trips to the base library, which was funded by the

California State Library. Base news was transmitted by way of the cleverly named weekly *Fly Paper* and monthly *Air Currents*, the latter describing itself as a "nonpolitical, nonsectarian, non-agitating and none-of-your-business publication."[48] In addition to straight news, both publications included an assortment of in-house cartoons, as well as advertisements from local

Mather Field's base publication, *Air Currents*, was known for its literary depth and artistic covers. *Center for Sacramento History.*

businesses. Music also was common. Mather's marching band gave daily concerts near the headquarters building, and a jazz band comprising one piano, two banjos, two violins, one saxophone and one tap drum made regular performances.

The war's end sent Mather into quick retrenchment. Starting on January 1, 1919, most officers were moved to other stations, and all cadets were sent to March Field, Riverside County, to complete their training, leaving a once-bustling Mather with a skeleton crew of two hundred. Despite the best efforts of the chamber and city, county and state officials, the school's days were numbered. The chamber's own J.W. Wooldridge called the school "a tottering institution" that was "ready prey to politicians."[49] His words were prescient as Congress—looking toward peacetime priorities—had little interest in funding Mather or most other aviation schools that had done such meaningful work in 1918.

By the time Mather was inactivated in 1922, five different aero squadrons had been stationed there: 28th, 200th, 201st, 283rd and 294th. Of course, nearly every plane that had been flown there—with the exception of a few Jennies and all the base's De Havilland DH-4 day bombers that arrived near the end of the war—had been constructed at Liberty Iron Works. Based on the War Department's lofty U.S. Air Corps goals and Liberty's $18 million contract, the factory was expected to produce 5 planes a day and 150 in a month.

Liberty's chief engineer was John A. Jordan, identified by a local publication as "one of the best technical engineers in aeroplane construction in the United States."[50] In mid-October 1917, Jordan and his ten-man engineering and production team were transferred to Sacramento from the Curtiss Aeroplane Company's Buffalo, New York location. Within hours of their arrival, Jordan, his team and Liberty's president, James M. Henderson, were fêted at a luncheon on the chamber's dime at the Hotel Land on Tenth and K Streets. The next day, architects were affixed to their drafting tables, developing schematics for Liberty's assembly sheds, and by October 23, construction had started on the parts for the concern's first series of Jennies.

Liberty's completed Jennies were moved to Mather and points beyond by way of rail, in most cases along Southern Pacific lines. In the name of efficiency, from December 1917 to March 22, SP and every other rail interest in the county was placed under the control of the United States Railroad Administration (USRA), making it one of the first times in American history that a major industry had been nationalized. While under USRA control, SP's Sacramento shops hardly lost their legendary edge, constructing 53 locomotives, 2,750 freight cars and 50 cabooses. As for the transport of JN-

Charles Virden's efforts with the Sacramento Consolidated Chamber of Commerce and acquisition of Mather and Liberty changed the destiny of Sacramento. *Sacramento Public Library.*

Shown is Globe Iron Works just prior to its 1917 conversion to Liberty. Del Paso Boulevard runs in the foreground. *Center for Sacramento History.*

4s from Liberty to Mather, planes were pushed out by way of a Western Pacific–controlled spur that ran right onto Liberty grounds. From there, the cars would make their way to the primary east–west SP line and then the dedicated SP and county-built spur to Mather.

Fearing sabotage, the factory was placed under the watchful eye of the National Guard soon after opening in October. Concerns were heightened after a December 1917 phone call made to the *Sacramento Star* by "a man with a distinct German accent," who claimed "that 18 machinists had walked out of the works, because non-union men were being employed."[51] While the accusations were proven to be false, the call nonetheless piqued Liberty's level of vigilance. It is also notable that Liberty claimed to employ no ethnic Germans, which, based on the climate of fear and the industry's vital importance, should hardly come as a surprise. From the outset, Liberty made it clear that "every man and woman seeking employment in the works [would] be scrutinized most carefully," reviewing "much of their past history, including places where employed and other data."[52]

By late autumn, it appeared that Liberty was truly on its way, possessing a momentum that came from its position at one of the American West's

Liberty workers construct the fuselage of a JN-4. The region's spruce stands were an essential medium for building the trainer. *Center for Sacramento History.*

primary rail hubs, as well as an ideal proximity to the Sierra Nevada's millions of stands of spruce, the wood of choice for constructing the JN-4. Yet a series of production delays, none of which was truly the company's fault, was an albatross Liberty could never truly shake. As contracted builders of the JN-4-D—the most advanced version of the Jenny—Jordan's team (not to mention other manufacturers) was sent both incomplete and incorrect blueprints for the model by both Curtiss and the Bureau of Aircraft Production (BAP). In lieu of simply correcting the mistake, Curtiss decided to dispatch sample planes to Liberty and the other affected factories to aid in production. Albeit a Jenny, manufacturers received the obsolete JN-4-A, as opposed to the JN-4-D. Once all had been sorted out in April 1918—a full six months after opening—Liberty was producing three planes a day. During that crucial six-month period, however, Liberty's more than eight hundred employees had not been idle, blazing ahead with crafting wooden parts for wings and fuselages. To cap Liberty's travails, it was discovered that, after the Armistice, the government sold two Liberty-made Jennies to Curtiss without going through the mandated bidding process and for a price that was well below what Liberty would have been willing to pay. Curtiss then went on to resell the planes at a profit. Although Liberty claimed that preferential treatment had been given to the larger manufacturer, it was still willing to enter into any future plane contract with the government, provided that the

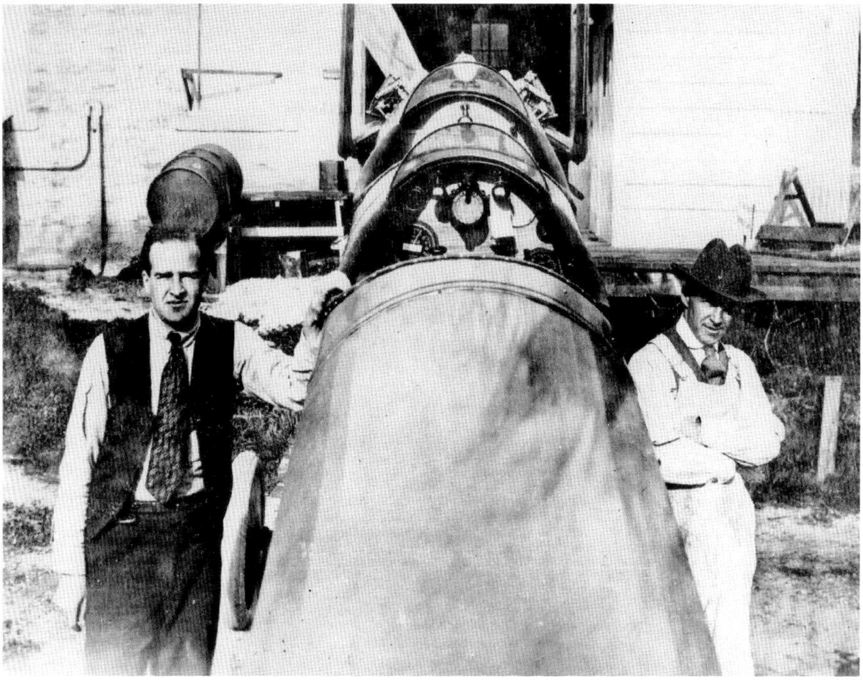

Curtiss engineers pose by the unfinished fuselage of a JN-4. Liberty-built trainers were well regarded by Mather's cadets and instructors. *Center for Sacramento History.*

company was afforded the "opportunities and privileges the same as granted other manufacturers."[53]

Of the three hundred planes that the government had contracted the factory to build, it was for the reasons already cited that Liberty was able to furnish only two hundred, and still the company could hang its hat on a quality effort. Liberty was never censured for quality control, and Mather instructor Captain Thomas Voss called the company's JN-4-D's "the best machines we had on Mather Field" for "they would fly better and were more solidly put together."[54] It is also worthy of mention that the nearly thirty thousand hours of flight time logged by Mather cadets (on mostly Liberty-made JN-4s) was the most of any stateside training school, a figure that is especially impressive when considering that Mather also had the fewest number of accidents. Nonetheless, with the Great War at an end and government contracts nowhere to be found, Liberty simply had no place to go. A peacetime posture of manufacturing both trucks and tractors was explored, but it was nothing that the concern was able to sustain.

The Mather-Liberty dynamic brings into focus what essential relationships are built between public and private interests when a nation descends into the throes of total war. Great War Sacramento viewed the duo as a point of civic pride. The dual responsibility of training aviators and constructing their airplanes meant: 1) the war had never been as close as it was now and 2) Sacramentans could make a day-to-day impact on its outcome. Liberty may have quickly faded into the fogs of history, but the region's love affair with Mather—stoked by the grand efforts of chamber head Arthur Dudley in the 1920s, '30s and '40s—endured well into the twentieth century.

3

BREAD BULLETS WILL WIN THE WAR

By Amanda G. DeWilde

Before the "European war" reached Sacramento, the region was on the cusp of an agricultural boom. Reclamation work added fertile bottomlands to thousands of acres of alluvial plains. Sacramento Valley boosters beckoned small farmers with "a hundred thousand acres of the richest soil in the world reclaimed and made ready for intensive husbandry."[55] Speculators sold pricey plots in new colonies throughout the area, including planned agricultural suburbs like Orange Vale (1887), Fair Oaks (1900), Carmichael colonies (1909), Rio Linda (1910), Citrus Heights (1910), Arcade Park (1911) and the Natomas Basin (1915). Sacramentans grew hops, almonds, asparagus, grapes, pears, cherries, figs, olives, peaches, potatoes, strawberries and tomatoes; they raised prize-winning hogs and poultry. They established a promising canning industry with the September 1913 opening of the $750,000 Libby, McNeil & Libby Fruit and Vegetable Cannery on Stockton Boulevard, the largest of its kind in the world. At the intersection of two transcontinental steam railroads, Sacramento was the distributing point of Central and Northern California's bounty and was looking forward to international trade through the new Panama Canal. The recently approved Port of Sacramento survey was also in the works, and the Yolo Causeway linking West Sacramento and Davis had just opened in 1916.

Across the Atlantic, agricultural production and distribution were hit hard within months of the outbreak of war in 1914. The continent was

A bucolic scene on a small suburban farm in Carmichael, one of several thousand just outside the city in 1918. *Sacramento Public Library.*

starving, and food had become as vital as munitions. Europe and Russia had been chief importers and exporters of food worldwide prior to the war, but the Allies and Central Powers alike quickly mounted huge deficits in agricultural production after the conflict began. Prices and demand rose as a result of blockades, invasions, the disorganization of shipping and a depleted labor force. Sugar, grains and dairy products became scarce. The Germans languished under Britain's strict naval blockade, with hundreds of thousands dying from starvation. Europe turned to the rest of the world to feed it.

Sacramento-area farmers were at first unsure about how the European war might drive values and shift demand. With exports in danger of being seized as contraband of war, Sacramentans had to unload them domestically or on weak European markets through England, the only nation in Europe still open to trade. War also put a hold on valuable public works projects like the construction of the Port of Sacramento and the extension of the state capitol complex. Others saw profit in how Sacramento might help in the war effort. U.S. support had increased the demand and value of some staples grown locally, and Sacramento farmers tentatively explored increasing production in order to export new goods like rice, barley, dried vegetables and fruits and canned goods.

Days before the United States declared war on Germany, the Sacramento Valley Development Association, a strong booster of colonization, adopted the slogan: "Increased crops from Sacramento valley farms to meet impending national needs." The association worked to colonize reclaimed land with settlers from eastern states, and its secretary, W.A. Beard of Oroville, saw opportunity in supporting the Allied nations. "This looks like a time when the Sacramento valley may rise to national need with profit to all concerned," he said.[56] At Beard's behest, Dean Thomas Forsyth Hunt of the University of California Department of Agriculture called a conference of experts to give recommendations for increasing food production on April 3, 1917. The conference took place at the 1,100-acre University Farm in Davis, a relatively new extension of the University of California. In attendance were many representatives from the University of California College of Agriculture, Dean H.E. Van Norman of the University Farm School and Sacramento's new county farm advisor, Carl J. Williams. The group recommended growing grain sorghum and Sudan grass for livestock feed and planting beans between trees in orchards.[57]

That same afternoon in Washington, President Woodrow Wilson requested that Congress declare war on Germany. Days later, he communicated the value of agricultural workers as fellow soldiers in the war on autocracy: "The farmers who devote their thought and their energy to this will be serving the country and conducting the fight for peace and freedom just as truly as the men on the battlefields and in the trenches."[58]

With the declaration of war on Germany on April 6, California responded with great alacrity. Before the war, America fed 110 million people; now, the country was required to feed more than twice as many mouths to help fuel the Allied forces. All local interests were made subservient to national demands, and the newly formed California State Council of Defense set policy. California "War Governor" William D. Stephens formed the Committee on Resources and Food Supply, with University of California president Benjamin Ide Wheeler as chair, to tackle the pressing issue of state preparedness. Agricultural representatives from throughout the state met to discuss how they would organize their efforts to stimulate food production. By the end of April 1917, the committee had completed a rapid agricultural survey of the entire state by way of public hearings held in nearly every county. At Sacramento's hearing on April 21 in Judge Malcolm C. Glenn's office, Dean Van Norman estimated that fifty thousand acres of fertile land

Uncle Sam bounds toward Europe with a basket of baked goods in Sacramento High School student Herb Phillips's cartoon. *Sacramento Public Library.*

could be cultivated in the county, granted that labor and machinery were made available.[59]

The "Food Crisis" was again the theme of the University Farm picnic and open house a week later, which enjoyed a record attendance of close to twenty thousand people. B.B. Meek, a member of the State Council of Defense, declared in his keynote talk that the state's greatest contribution to the cause was food and that "bread bullets will win the war."[60] While the enthusiasm was there in the first few weeks of the war, food production goals were rather vague and disorganized, with a general request to produce more meat, eggs, butter and milk.

Sacramento's efforts toward both food production and conservation gained focus upon passage of the Food and Fuel Control Act of August 10, 1917, which created Herbert C. Hoover's United States Food Administration and the Food Production Act, administered by David F. Houston. The Food Production Act appropriated $11 million to stimulate production and boost education at the local level in California. This included surveying food production, management and pricing, dealing with pests and disease, purchasing seeds and educating farmers and lay people alike on food production and conservation primarily through Farm Bureaus and universities.

Thomas F. Hunt's College of Agriculture would work closely with the State Council of Defense to carry out the federal mandate, and the university threw in an additional budget of $605,000 behind research, instruction and especially agricultural extension. In addition, California received $104,000 per annum from the Emergency Food Production Act for food demonstrations through county Farm Bureaus, $20,000 of which was allotted for female demonstrators.[61] The State Food Administration also set production goals. At the outset, California was asked to increase wheat production by 20 percent, and other targets followed.

Sacramento County farm advisor Carl J. Williams applied the state recommendations at the local level. He headed the Sacramento County Farm Bureau, which was founded in January 1917 with eleven farm centers scattered across the county. The bureau dedicated itself to the interests of small farmers and the issue of colonization in addition to increased food production. Williams had a passion for education and devoted a large portion of his time to boys' and girls' agricultural clubs. He set up forty-three different clubs in Sacramento County, teaching everything from the practicality of keeping pigs to the growing of vegetables on small farms. Girls were educated to "carry on the work that devolves upon wives of ranchers," while the boys were taught the "real farm work."[62] Some girls' clubs took a more active role. Williams helped establish the first girls' canning club in the state at San Juan Union High School. The group planted, harvested and canned one and a half acres of peas, and they enthusiastically performed their own songs and stage stunts to promote their work, including a new version of "Over There":

Over there, over there, send the word, over there,
That the girls are planting,
The boys are ranting,
The girls are "planting" everywhere,
So prepare, do not stare, you'll see them, from now on, everywhere,
They are working,
And they're not shirking,
And they won't give up, 'till it's over, over there.[63]

Beyond the Farm Bureau, the greatest sharing of new ideas and technologies took place at exhibitions and demonstrations. While the theme of the 1915 Panama-Pacific International Exposition in San Francisco was "History of the Arts of Peace in a World at War," both the 1917 and 1918 California State Fairs held in the capital city had a decidedly different theme: more food for the war. The U.S. Food Administration provided a complete exhibit on food conservation for the 1917 fair, and every educational display and demonstration had food production and conservation as its principal purpose. In service of conservation, scrap metal was melted down for bullets after stuntwoman Helen Holmes leapt from a moving engine during the traditional locomotive collision on the last day. Over eight days, a record 250,000 people attended the state's first wartime fair. Patriotism, Profit and Pleasure were the three notes of the next year's fair, and agricultural production and conservation again pervaded every exhibit, "Everywhere among the vast exhibits is a warlike touch, reminding the people that this great empire is now straining every sinew to raise vast stores of foodstuffs and send them across the seas to feed our soldiers and our allies."[64]

Tractors were a big draw at both fairs. With horses scarce and efficiency the word of the day, farmers began to embrace mechanization during the war. "When I saw that tractor coming, it was to laugh," recalled W.G. Smith of Sacramento, who had a new Wallis tractor brought to his river ranch for a demonstration in July 1918.[65] War brought the tractor from "a pretty good thing that every farmer hoped to have 'sometime' [to] a necessary thing that every farmer must have 'now.'"[66] Farmers who adopted mechanization were able to cultivate and transport food more efficiently. At the Cutter Bros. peach orchards outside Courtland, the autotruck driver delivered five to six loads of fruit to the cannery, compared with fewer than one and a half with a wagon. E.G. Cutter's sixteen-year-old son safely and quickly hauled five loads of shipping fruit per day on an 1,800-pound truck.[67] The California Tractor and Implement Association took out an ad in the April 1917 *California Cultivator*

A war-themed 1918 California State Fair poster pictures Sacramento's military and agricultural might. *California State Library*.

announcing its first annual demonstration and declared that "to see and study this equipment and to learn the profits and possibilities in tractor farming is a patriotic duty and a profit-making opportunity for every farmer."[68]

Smarter farming and mechanization would increase efficiency, but more labor was needed to fill the void left by young men going to war. The call for increased production brought the agricultural labor shortage to the forefront. Northern California farmers met with state officials in Sacramento on May 11, 1917, to discuss how to recruit more labor. Sacramento River Delta farmers in attendance hinted toward acquiring foreign labor in an appeal they sent to the State Council of Defense:

> *Resolved, that the farmers of this State assembled in mass meeting in Sacramento find it impossible to increase production, without immediate and large supply of farm help the scarcity of farm workers in placing our normal crop in jeopardy and that labor accustomed to farm work must be brought to California from such sources as have a large population of people capable of doing agricultural work.*[69]

Arthur Seymour of Sacramento reported that the farms of the Delta region were absolutely dependent on Japanese, Indian and Chinese labor. Delta farmers preferred foreign workers because of their strong work ethic and cleanliness. But Judge Peter J. Shields, chairman of the Sacramento County Council of Defense, warned against importing foreign workers: "Our Orchard may as well be in Japan if we don't support the white man." U.S. commissioner of immigration Edward White of San Francisco was also in attendance and confirmed that the current exclusion laws would not be changed. He encouraged the use of young men and women for lighter farm work along with better conditions and wages for men.

Sacramento agriculturalist Simon J. Lubin, president of the State Commission of Immigration and Housing, agreed. Lubin's dedication to agricultural policy extended beyond U.S. borders when he helped found the International Institute of Agriculture at Rome in 1908. And during the war years, he provided key input on increasing production for starving countries like Ukraine. Lubin argued that America alone was capable of feeding Allied nations and recommended that all U.S. states contribute a "Liberty Crop" as a "freewill offering" to the United States government and to the Allies. His State Commission of Immigration and Housing was formed to deal with conditions that led to the Wheatland hop field riot of 1913 and reported in May 1917 that the importation, even for a set period, of foreign immigrants from China or Mexico would only aggravate racial tensions and drive down wages. The commission strongly opposed importing foreign labor to solve the problem. It blamed the dearth of good workers on inadequate wages, poor labor camp conditions and the lack of a central clearinghouse for labor intelligence.[70]

Opposition to Asian labor was an outgrowth of a growing push-back by Progressives against cheaper tenant farming in the Sacramento River Delta. While Progressive speculators like D.W. Carmichael were straining to attract small farmers to pricey new suburban colonies in Sacramento, by 1915, 75 percent of land in the Delta region was operated by tenants, 76 percent of whom were Japanese. Japanese-run farms in California grew from 81,903 acres in 1910 to 436,141 acres in 1920.[71] In an earlier attempt to stem the flow of foreign landowners into California, state attorney general Ulysses S. Webb had authored the California Alien Land Law of 1913 (Webb-Haney Act), which passed by an overwhelming majority and prohibited the ownership of land by aliens for more than three years. But in the midst of the wartime labor shortage, the newly formed Japanese Agricultural Association of California asked for changes to the bill to allow it to "participate more effectively and extensively in the war activities of the American Government and people." The association adopted a resolution calling for the changes at a conference at the California State Fair in September 1918.[72] A new California Alien Land Law passed again in 1920 and was amended in 1923, but the Land Laws remained in place until 1952, when they were ruled in violation of the equal protection clause of the Fourteenth Amendment to the United States Constitution.

With foreign labor off the table, Sacramento conducted a brief experiment recruiting homeless men. During raids made in the city by chief of police Ira Conran in early 1918, several hundred homeless men were arrested and about eighty given the opportunity to avoid jail if they would work on local ranches.[73] The men reportedly could not be induced to work. Area farms finally decided on two sources of alternative labor: the Boys' Working Reserve and the Women's Land Army.

The U.S. Department of Labor identified the nation's young men as a significant untapped labor pool in 1917, when it was estimated that 5 million were in school or employed in "unproductive occupations." An agreement between the U.S. Department of Agriculture and U.S. Department of Labor formed the Boys' Working Reserve in the fall of that year. Squads of city boys between sixteen and twenty-one years of age took to work on farms, staying at work camps or in family farmhouses. The California State Board of Education drew 2,158 boys and 541 girls willing to accept employment from 142 high schools, and 375 boys enrolled in the United States Boys' Working Reserve in Sacramento County. Sacramento boys were sent out on farms during the summer and on Saturdays to pick fruit under the supervision of teachers. They received certificates of enlistment from the federal government and were given bronze badges after three weeks of work. The program was so successful locally that a large-scale mobilization camp was planned in Davis but did not come to fruition before the war ended.

Sacramento found even more success in recruiting women for lighter farm work. Inspired by the success of recruiting women for agricultural work in France, England and Canada, the United States finally mobilized women for farm labor by establishing the Women's Land Army (WLA) in 1918. On May 19, 1918, the Northern California Division of the Women's Land Army began recruiting for able-bodied women ages eighteen and older to do light agricultural labor at area farms. Mrs. Hugh Bradford was appointed honorary chairman for the Sacramento WLA. A recruiting office opened at the courthouse, and Mrs. A.H. DeGaston did the work of enrolling women.[74] Rosabella Best of *Pacific Rural Press* reported that the WLA would need women with "physical endurance, determination, and faithfulness of service to prove the quality of American womanhood in this crisis."[75]

The Sacramento office had no problem finding recruits, with more than 175 young women enlisting in the office during the first month. On June 5, the *Sacramento Bee* announced the arrival of the WLA; a few women were assigned to Libby, McNeil & Libby Cannery, and another group was to pick fruit at Casselli Ranch near "Fruit Ridge." A few weeks later, a group went to West Sacramento to work in bean fields on a large river ranch, chaperoned by Miss Anna E. Applegate. District farmers appreciated the young women's hard work and, in addition to increased wages, treated them to a freezer of ice cream.[76] A group of fifty women and girls, headed by E.H. Traxler, composed the city's first full unit. They traveled to Florin and Lodi in August 1918 to work in the vineyards, picking grapes and enjoying "sanitary" camps with "first-class cooking."[77] Although late in coming, the WLA supplied a dependable source of labor to Sacramento farms and canneries during the last summer of the war.

Apart from a labor shortage, foes to food production in the Sacramento area included pests, sabotage and frost. Sacramento farmers fought the dangerous red spider, which attacked almond, prune and young pear trees, and they made an enemy of the dreaded ground squirrel. The State Commission of Horticulture and State Farm Bureau declared "Squirrel Week" from April 29 to May 4, 1918, and offered cash prizes to students who could slay the most rodents.

Through a cooperative effort, 104,509 ground squirrels perished that week. Students from San Juan Union High School killed the most squirrels in Sacramento County, earning a thirty-dollar second prize. Sacramento was serious about rodent control; District Attorney Hugh B. Bradford placed thirteen liens on property in the Haggin Grant in Sacramento for failing to comply with the squirrel ordinance. Unfortunately, strategies like

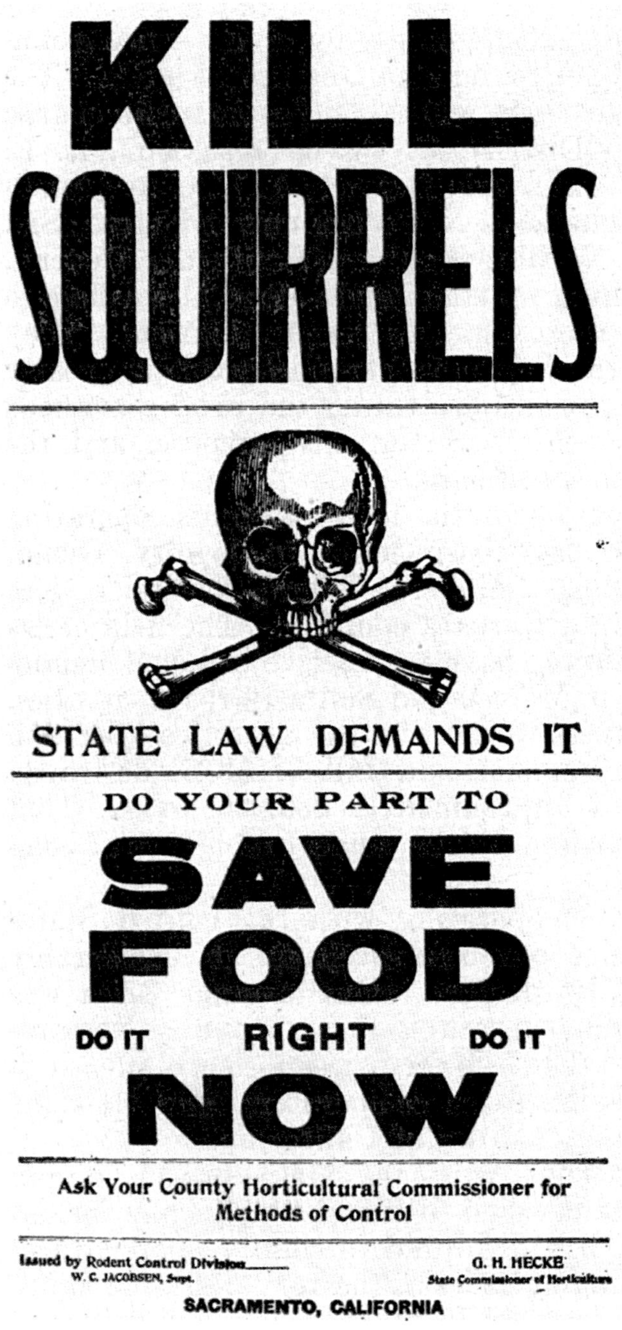

A grim poster from the California Department of Horticulture's 1918 anti-squirrel campaign. *Sacramento Public Library.*

exploding waste balls soaked in carbon disulfide in the squirrel holes may have led to local fires in the vicinity of Folsom Prison and Mormon Island.

Farmers also feared sabotage by resident enemies or German agents. In June 1918, guards were posted at the request of the State Council of Defense to protect grain fields and were instructed to shoot to kill any person caught trying to set fire to the fields. The state also issued a bulletin in January 1918 warning of German agents distributing powerful, poisonous pollen to destroy the state's wheat crop.

A spring frost in the 1917 growing season also threatened crops. In contrast, 1918 was an ideal year. Robert E. Jones, editor of the California Country Life Department at the *Sacramento Bee*, delightedly reported in July 1918 that "if Uncle Sam were like the Kaiser in asserting a partnership with God, he could claim co-operation of the Almighty with much better grace than Wilhelm, for the season has been almost ideal for the growing of large crops."

By the end of the war, Sacramento agriculture had been reenergized—arable land, production and related industry all increased. California had sent more foodstuffs to the Allies, by population, than any other state—valued at more than $1,000,000 daily, according to Ralph Merritt, food administrator for California. Sacramento County went from 275,682 acres of improved land in farms in 1910 to 399,024 acres in 1920. The number of farms increased from 1,601 to 2,975 over that period, and the value of all crops more than quadrupled, from $4,720,010 to $19,845,558.[78]

Sacramento secured a number of very lucrative contracts with Allied armies. A representative from the British Purchasing Company spent $4,000,000 during the month of July 1917 in California, mostly in the Sacramento and San Joaquin Valleys, buying 100,000 tons of barley to add to the Allies' food supply. Libby, McNeill & Libby received one of the largest orders of the war: to secure the British army with $400,000 worth of canned goods, including packed fruits, vegetables and meats. The contract was secured by Major Z.A. Hay with the Quartermaster Department of the Australian army. The *Sunday Leader* hailed the agreement: "Sacramento, through the contract, is coming into her own, also by the recognition of this city as one of the centers for the production of foods."[79] Libby, McNeill & Libby expanded further in Sacramento with the construction of a new asparagus plant in Locke. The company also built a condensed milk plant in Sacramento following the success of a similar plant in Galt.

The Sacramento Valley nearly doubled its production of grain for any season during the previous fifteen years. Joseph Arnold of the Phoenix Milling Company optimistically proclaimed, "The enormous yield of wheat

Several large combine harvesters use horsepower to transport wheat to Sperry Flour Mill in 1917. *Center for Sacramento History.*

and barley is veritably flooding the valley with gold...and the measure of prosperity is going to be unbounded."[80] Sacramento was able to harvest eleven to fifteen sacks of wheat per acre, versus the ordinary six to eight, and enjoyed similar gains in barley. The cultivation of rice took off most dramatically, from fifteen thousand acres in 1914 to eighty-three thousand by 1917. The value of the crop exploded from $75,000 in 1912 to $14,000,000 in 1918. Phillips Rice Milling Company invested in a five-story rice mill at Front and P Streets. Sacramento also planted 30 percent more acreage in beans for the 1917 season, and the Sacramento Dock and Warehouse Company constructed the largest bean-cleaning and storage plant on the Pacific Coast in West Sacramento. Eastern states drained California of fruit, offering higher rates for the supply. Sacramento sent record amounts of peaches, pears and grapes east via the Pacific Fruit Express; 133 refrigerated rail cars passed through the city on a single day in August 1918.

While the agricultural industry did its part to boost production, Sacramentans reclaimed their backyards and public lands for war gardens, with most of the garden soldiers being children. The United States Garden Army of Schoolchildren was formed in March 1918 at the behest of the

National Emergency Food Garden Commission. Harry Snell, director of manual training for the Sacramento School District, requested that schools train thirteen thousand Sacramento students in backyard farming and asked every lot owner to tell the nearest principal about land children could garden. City schools superintendent Charles S. Hughes, who was supportive of the effort, labored to put every child to work on the increased production of foodstuffs. Soon, small war gardens began sprouting up at nearly every school in the county.

Students took advantage of any available public lands. In the city, teachers directed students in cultivating blocks assigned to their schools. One such garden was Ms. Lucy Hinkson's war garden along H between Twenty-seventh and Twenty-eighth Streets, tended by students from Mary J. Watson Grammar School. Another was located on two vacant city blocks opposite the state capitol (about 8.00 acres) and converted by 100 schoolboys into a popcorn war garden on May 18, 1918. The output of the city school gardens was substantial. More than 3,400 students cultivated 50.85 acres in the city and produced $30,000 of food in 1918.

War gardens also made their way into new school plans. When San Juan Union High School's new building opened in 1915, state gardener William Vortriede gave advice on the outdoor grounds and blocked out space for play, flowers and experimental gardening. City commissioner D.W. Carmichael likewise consulted with the state landscape architect to design Carmichael School's war garden along artistic and scientific lines in 1918. That year, Carmichael tried to establish a municipal garden growing produce that would be split between orphanages and the city jail, a move that the *Caterpillar Times* called "a real act of conservation and greater production to cooperate with the nation's program of economy for the remainder of the war."[81]

Folsom Prison even contributed to the effort. Headed by practical farmer George Fleckenstein, a crew of sixty convicts cleared forty acres for cultivation, bringing the total to more than two hundred acres of barley, oats, alfalfa, potatoes, onions and vegetables. Convicts also developed a poultry department and raised 220 hogs.

In addition to increasing production at all levels, Sacramento signed up to conserve food. Work in this area shifted mostly to housewives and restaurants, who were creative in their solutions to the food problem. After passage of the Emergency Food Production Act in August 1917, Herbert Hoover reported on how the nation should scale back consumption to sustain the Allies with meats, fats, sugar and grains. He inaugurated a national food-saving campaign on August 1, 1917. Housewives were

Students from Mary J. Watson Grammar School break ground on a new war garden. *California State Library*.

asked to contribute to the war effort through eliminating waste, making substitutions and rationing. Local newspapers first published food pledges beginning in early July. Housewives signed a card agreeing to abide by the rulings of the food administrator, and Sacramento women began by pledging one meatless day each week and one wheatless meal each day. Judge Peter J. Shields headed up the food pledge campaign for the City and County of Sacramento, receiving more than twenty thousand signatures from area housewives by early November. Chamber of commerce president Harry S. Maddox became Sacramento City and County food administrator with the task of enforcing the new food-conservation regulations. Sacramento families, who were already struggling with high food prices, worked hard to conserve. They scrimped, saved, canned and instituted a "clean plate plan," disposing of scraps to chickens and rabbits and leaving garbage men with little business.

Local newspapers did their part by publishing columns like food administrator Merritt's "Official Food News," along with "The Housewive's Section" by Charlotte P. Ebbet, California director of home economics, and the two-panel cartoon *Swatting the Food Slacker*, with the subtitle: "Everett

True, noted patriot, joins United States Food Administration in drive on conservation shirkers."

Businesses also dedicated themselves to conservation. In August 1917, T. Franker of the Travelers Hotel in Sacramento adopted beefless Fridays and Mondays, and the *Sacramento Bee* reported on the possible introduction of whale meat in area eateries. Allan Pollock, head of Southern Pacific Railroad dining and restaurants, committed the food service to the Hoover pledge in October.[82] Area hotels joined him in trying to meet Hoover's call for less wheat bread, beef, mutton, pork, milk, fats and sugar. By November, twenty-six restaurants and hotels had pledged meatless Tuesdays, including the Hotel Sacramento, Hotel Land, Sutter Club, Hart's Lunch Counters and Rosemount Grill. Local ice cream dealers complied with the request for "ice cream–less Thursdays," which later became "Sweetless Days"—only partially followed the first time around because the cards reportedly did not make it to the printer in time.[83] Even local clubs and organizations cut back. Mrs. A.A. Goddard, Sacramento chairman of the Women's Committee of the State Council of Defense, called for local groups to "Hooverize" meals and put an end to "showy eating."[84]

Some Sacramentans found inventive ways to conserve. With wheat as the first to go, local bakers scrambled for substitutes. Phoenix Milling Company began using barley as a wheat substitute, housewives swapped out wheat for barley in breakfast cereals and the chamber of commerce looked into establishing a "Barley Day" in the city. German-born real estate agent Paul H. Steude, Sacramento's "world's champion small farmer," was one of many nationwide to seek out a solution to the wheat shortage. He introduced the use of potato flour in the United States and fashioned his new "war bread" using potato starch made from waste potatoes and peelings from local restaurants. In July 1917, Steude wrote to the State Board of Control and Governor Stephens of his invention and was invited to test it by installing a plant at the Napa State Hospital.[85]

"Liberty Bread" made its Sacramento debut in December 1917. It was described by J.S. Goldie, local baker and recently appointed leader of Section 9 of the War Emergency Organization of the Baker Industry, as having an "altogether different flavor" due to a reduction in extra ingredients like sugar, milk and shortening. The housewife and her family would need to "adjust their palates to the new flavor and think of Uncle Sam and Liberty."[86] In addition to cooking and baking with substitutes, canning took off in popularity as a way to preserve perishable fruits and vegetables year round. Sacramento housewives found easy ways to can using the simple one-period cold-pack method, which required only a wash boiler and a few cans or jars.

Some took advantage of the patriotism and desperation of many Californians. Leo J. Wortheimer of San Francisco sold the "Butter Merger" extensively to Sacramentans, claiming it could produce two pounds of butter from one pound of milk and one pound of butter. The State Board of Health shut down businesses that sold Wortheimer's merger, and he later was fined $250 by the State Bureau of Foods and Drugs.

Those who failed to follow regulations regarding food waste, substitution or rationing were heavily penalized. For restaurants, an emergency ordinance by the City of Sacramento made it unlawful "to destroy or permit the destruction of, or to render unfit for human or animal consumption, any food of the original value of twenty-five dollars or more."[87]

The first restaurant closed in Sacramento under the regulations of food administrator Harry Maddox was the Japanese-owned Sun restaurant at 408 J Street. Maddox declared the May 1918 closure to be but a start in the local drive against violating regulations for food conservation. In August, the local bakers' committee made recommendations to food commissioner Ralph Merritt to close bakeries that refused to use substitutes for wheat flour. Several bakers went on trial before a food jury at the chamber of commerce on charges of failing to use enough substitutes and to make correct reports to Washington. While most bakers received warnings, Harry Kupas of the Superior Bakery had to close his doors for one month for failing to follow the rules.

Food restrictions became more austere as the war carried on. By May 1918, state food commissioner Merritt had labeled any person who ate wheat at that time "either a slacker or a crank." He banned whipped cream from homes, public eating houses, clubs and hospitals a few months later because of its high butter fat. Sacramento food administrator Maddox restricted Sacramentans to two pounds of sugar per month in June (three pounds allowed for boardinghouses and camps, mines and remote ranches), and he requested that all area churches have a sermon on food conservation on Sunday, June 2. By October, he had deemed teas and banquets unnecessary, condemning them as "fourth meals." Maddox additionally outlined twelve strict food conservation rules for public eating places directed toward saving bread, cereals, meat, fat, sugar, coffee, dairy products and rice. The list included rules like: "No bacon shall be served as a garnisher" and "Food shall not be burned and all waste shall be saved to feed animals or reduced to obtain fat."[88]

In November 1918, Hoover asked Americans to continue sacrificing in order to feed Europe until the next harvest in 1919—even going so far as saying that the nation would need to supply 60 percent of the world's food supply. However, many food restrictions were lifted immediately after hostilities ended. The use of "war bread" and the sugar ban ended in November 1918, and most other restrictions were lifted within the next month, continuing with the decline and formal dissolution of the U.S. Food Administration in the spring of 1921.

Food did win the war, and Sacramento's food soldiers were integral. The war years both before and after U.S. involvement presented Sacramento farmers and eaters with a great challenge—a challenge that it met through education, mechanization, ingenuity and hard work. By the end of the war, the city was poised to take on new challenges with rapidly expanding industry and infrastructure.

4

WITH ENTHUSIASM, INTELLIGENCE AND ABILITY

By Amanda G. DeWilde

On the evening of October 9, 1918, thousands of Sacramento women marched through the city's business district to raise subscriptions for the Fourth Liberty Loan. Dressed in white, bond sellers held fifteen-cent Japanese lanterns on slender rods high above their heads and bore headbands reading, "Buy More Bonds." The river of women in white and lines of lantern light were broken up by colorful banners representing each division of war workers, marching to patriotic tunes. Captains of the Liberty Loan workers wore Goddess of Liberty headgear. Mothers bore armbands reading, "Navy," "Marines" or "Army" in honor of the service of their sons. With the Red Cross representing the largest contingent, all departments marched, from the seamstresses in white bonnets with their captains in red headgear to the nurses with "stiffly starched uniforms and neat caps." The Council of Defense division leaders presented white shields emblazoned with the words "Council of Defense" in gold letters and were followed by Catholic women's organizations, the YWCA, the Ladies' Auxiliary of Spanish War Veterans and the Jewish Women War Workers. Farther back was the Salvation Army and a popular Japanese division, along with descendants of all Allied nations. A group of city and county employees, teachers and hotel workers came next. At the end proudly marched women employed by the canneries and Women's Land Army workers from the hop fields, "clad in blue overalls and marching under an archway of hop vines."[89]

Southern Pacific Railway employees represent women's war work aboard a parade float, 1917. *Center for Sacramento History.*

The marchers raised thousands over the city's quota of $3 million for the final Liberty Bond drive and represented their contingents with pride. The spectacle provided a moving illustration of the breadth and depth of women's contributions to the war effort. It also demonstrated the incredible progress that had been made in mobilizing Sacramento's women in just eighteen months.

At the outset of U.S. involvement in World War I, the federal government recognized that the country would need to call on the whole population and effectively mobilize women throughout the country, both in traditional roles and in those vacated by men serving in the military. Women also would be needed to serve abroad in record numbers with the Red Cross and other support agencies. In recognizing the potential value of an organized female citizenry, President Woodrow Wilson formed the Women's Committee of the Council of National Defense in late April 1917 as a "clearing house for women's activities all over the United States." Its purpose was "to give patriotic inspiration" and "to furnish educational assistance."[90]

Suffrage movement founder Dr. Anna Howard Shaw headed the national group, while Mrs. Herbert A. Cable chaired the California Women's Committee, which was organized on May 28, 1917. The committee's areas of focus were a broad representation of the homefront effort: 1) registration for service; 2) home relief; 3) Allied relief; 4) food production, conservation, thrift; 5) Americanization; 6) labor of women; 7) public health; 8) child welfare; 9) instructive courses; 10) protective regulations, recreation; 11) conservation of moral and spiritual forces; and 12) special committee on Liberty Loan Fund.[91] Fourteen town units in Sacramento County fell under the command of Mrs. A.A. Goddard, who coordinated women's organizations. She also conducted a mass registration, asking every woman in the county to give her name, age, birthplace, physical condition, occupation and other data that would indicate the work she was best fitted to perform. Goddard appealed to the women of Sacramento and invited them to a patriotic mass meeting in July 1917:

> *While your sons and brothers are preparing to answer the call to fight at the front, it is fitting and proper that the women should associate themselves together in order that they may render aid and comfort in such an efficient manner that the boys who brave the dance of the sea and who meet the shot and shell of battle will fully realize that they have wide-awake mothers and sisters at home.*[92]

In an era when women exercised their influence outside the home through clubs and associations, the Women's Committee rallied the feminine population in this way. Sacramento women took a more active part in local groups whose activities were now devoted to the war effort. The Orangevale Women's Club was typical of others, directing its energies by spending the war years "learning to make war bread, preparing meatless meals and generally concentrating on economy in the home." The ladies resolved to "pledge themselves to raise garden produce and poultry, preserve as much as possible and even adopt a French girl whom they supported."[93]

Many of the Sacramento clubs tendered their service through the Women's Council, which formed out of the Tuesday Club in 1902 and brought together twenty-three area women's organizations, including the Courtland Farmers Club, Ladies Hebrew Benevolent Society, Native Daughters of the Golden West, Sacramento Woman's Christian Temperance Union, Kingsley Art Club and Women's Home Mission Society. Because they were focused on war projects, not too much was done on the council's own agenda. Instead, "winning the war came first." The club signed a petition of preparedness to "make the United States secure from foreign power" in early 1916 and wore buttons in support of this pledge. In 1917, the club invited Carl Williams to address club members on the subject of the farm labor shortage, urging that they release boys during vacation to join the Boys Working Reserve. And later that year, Mrs. H.F. Miles, president of the Woman's Council, delivered a lecture at the Sacramento High School auditorium dealing with women's work in the war and the activities of the Red Cross.[94]

Many clubs hosted speakers and offered training, some inviting speakers from France and Belgium to talk about their struggles and make the cause more tangible. Prominent local women joined the ranks of the "Four Minute Men" speakers, sharing speeches on topics furnished by the Committee on Public Information during reel changes at local movie theaters and at area schools, churches and businesses. One of the city's four-minute speakers was Valla E. Parkinson, an attorney who was the first woman admitted to practice in Sacramento. Like many women of the time, Parkinson was busy. On top of her law practice and speaking commitments, she claimed active membership in eight organizations during the war years in addition to her work on the Red Cross, Liberty Loan and other war efforts.[95]

Women interested in a more active role joined up with the Red Cross, contributing to the nonsectarian group's relief work at home and abroad. The Sacramento County Chapter was formed on April 9, 1917, with headquarters at 1010 Fourth Street. The chapter began with one hundred members and set a goal to recruit thousands. Moneys were quickly raised to aid the organization. Weinstock, Lubin & Co., its largest donor, pledged $3,034 in May 1917, with president S.W. McKim announcing that the store would contribute $2,500 plus $1 memberships for every employee.[96] Soon after that, the City of Sacramento levied a two-cent tax to add $14,000 to the effort. Women's clubs also held events (dances, dinners and parades) to fundraise for the Red Cross. The chapter itself launched a big drive to secure $112,500 for the Red Cross War Fund campaign with a grand march in May 1918. It solicited pledges and branded those who didn't sign as being "in the class of 'slackers.'"[97]

Once the Sacramento chapter was fully established, the Red Cross offered women a wide range of departments in which to serve. Women could sign up with the Sewing Branch, which sent mufflers, wristlets, sweaters and socks overseas. That branch took over the state capitol assembly chamber for its headquarters with the permission of George G. Radcliffe, superintendent of the state capitol grounds and building. They could also join the Canteen

Service and work at railroad stations handing soldiers sandwiches, fruits, nuts, postcards and other articles and gifts. The local Canteen Service served 87,608 men from June 10, 1918, to December 2, 1919. On one evening in August 1918, 1,200 soldiers in khaki traveling aboard twelve rail cars were showered with cigarettes, magazines, candies and fruits by members of the service at the Western Pacific railway station.[98] And Red Cross members could also teach—several members taught popular classes in hygiene, first aid, home nursing and dietetics after hours at Sacramento High School. All ten sections offered in October 1918 filled immediately after registration opened. The chapter even recruited for a girls' automobile corps, which delivered supplies around town.

A daring few signed up to serve as Red Cross nurses "somewhere in France." The national Red Cross called for twenty-five thousand nurses, and Sacramento was given a quota of fifty nurse recruits for the army, navy and Red Cross.[99] Finding unmarried women willing and able to serve was a challenge. Twenty-two nurses—graduates and those with four years' experience—were enrolled by the end of July 1917. They went through a physical examination and immunity treatment for typhoid and smallpox before standing ready for call. Properly trained nurses were at such a premium midway through the war that Sacramentans were asked to economize the use of nurses and take care of the sick at home when possible. The qualifications had relaxed a bit by the end of the war to draw in more numbers. In August 1918, the United States Student Nurse Reserves set up its headquarters at the Hotel Sacramento and offered prospective nurses a shortened two-year course load, after which they would serve a year in France or as rehabilitation nurses after the war.[100] Given that the program started that fall, the majority who registered likely ended up helping with the Spanish influenza epidemic that struck that October.

By October 1918, forty-five nurses from Sacramento had "joined the nation's manhood in the fight against autocracy," signing up with the army, navy and Red Cross. Eleven were serving in Europe, while others were stationed across the country, and ten who were not qualified for military duty worked as Home Defense nurses locally.[101] One of the eleven nurses serving in Europe was the intrepid Anastasia Miller, superintendent of nurses at Mater Misercordiae Hospital Training School in Sacramento. In the spring of 1918, she traveled to New York City to obtain her passport, get outfitted and board a ship bound for France. Miller went on to serve on the front lines in France through the end of World War I, working with refugees and treating wounded soldiers at an advanced dressing station. Her colorful

Anastasia Miller poses in her nurse's uniform, circa 1917. *Sacramento Public Library.*

letters written home to her parents and her brother Benjamin during her year of service offer an intimate look into the exciting and challenging work of Red Cross nurses on the western front.

After arriving in Paris in April 1918, Miller was immediately impressed by the mobilization of women there: "I've never known such fortitude. Every bit of work here is done by the women—freight and baggage handling, street sweeping, the entire car and train service, electricians, in fact no men can be found except in uniform." She first had charge of a refugee hospital

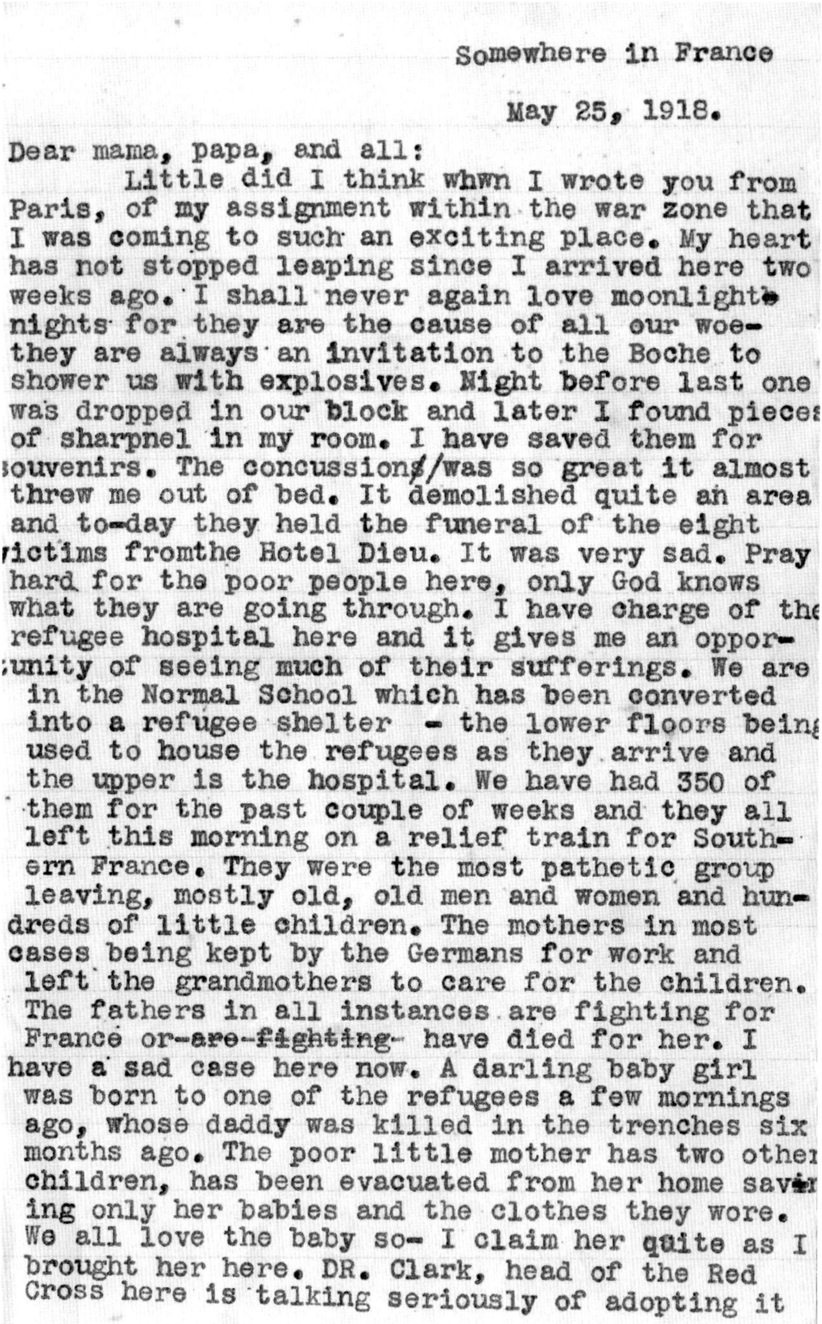

Somewhere in France

May 25, 1918.

Dear mama, papa, and all:

Little did I think whwn I wrote you from Paris, of my assignment within the war zone that I was coming to such an exciting place. My heart has not stopped leaping since I arrived here two weeks ago. I shall never again love moonlight nights for they are the cause of all our woe- they are always an invitation to the Boche to shower us with explosives. Night before last one was dropped in our block and later I found pieces of sharpnel in my room. I have saved them for souvenirs. The concussion~~s~~/was so great it almost threw me out of bed. It demolished quite an area and to-day they held the funeral of the eight victims fromthe Hotel Dieu. It was very sad. Pray hard for the poor people here, only God knows what they are going through. I have charge of the refugee hospital here and it gives me an oppor-tunity of seeing much of their sufferings. We are in the Normal School which has been converted into a refugee shelter - the lower floors being used to house the refugees as they arrive and the upper is the hospital. We have had 350 of them for the past couple of weeks and they all left this morning on a relief train for South-ern France. They were the most pathetic group leaving, mostly old, old men and women and hun-dreds of little children. The mothers in most cases being kept by the Germans for work and left the grandmothers to care for the children. The fathers in all instances are fighting for France or ~~are fighting~~ have died for her. I have a sad case here now. A darling baby girl was born to one of the refugees a few mornings ago, whose daddy was killed in the trenches six months ago. The poor little mother has two other children, has been evacuated from her home sav-ing only her babies and the clothes they wore. We all love the baby so- I claim her quite as I brought her here. DR. Clark, head of the Red Cross here is talking seriously of adopting it

In letters home to her parents and brother, Anastasia Miller described life as a Red Cross nurse on the front lines in France. *Sacramento Public Library.*

"somewhere in France," located in a Normal School that had been converted into a shelter for 350 refugees; the lower floors were for intake and housing, while the upper floors served as a hospital. She wrote to her parents of her thrilling work, "Little did I think whwn [*sic*] I wrote you from Paris, of my assignment within the war zone that I was coming to such an exciting place. My heart has not stopped leaping since I arrived here two weeks ago."[102]

Miller then worked at an advanced dressing station serving thousands of wounded soldiers from all Allied nations: Americans, French, British, Scottish ("with their little kilts") and colonial troops bearing every kind of wound inflicted by bombs, gas, shell, machine guns and shrapnel. She even wrote of dressing a man shot by an airplane from above (the bullet entered his ear and traveled down through his body). Shortly after the war ended, Miller was outfitted for an assignment in Archangel, Russia, for which she was eager to serve: "I was first and for a time the only one and was quite a popular heroine for they explained to me the long voyage, the six months darkness and the fact that I might have to eat candles and freeze to death but I told them I took the chance of being blown to pieces and that freezing hadn't nearly the horrors for me."[103] Miller was instead called to Southern France for the remainder of the war. As she witnessed the celebration of the Armistice in Paris attended by King George of Great Britain, King Albert of Belgium and Woodrow Wilson, she received news from home about the "awful story of the 'flu.'"

By the fall of 1918, the Spanish influenza epidemic had taken precedence over the war for nurses in Sacramento. The first cases were reported in early October and slowly increased to thirty-six (with eleven at Mather Field) by mid-month. Then the flu became an outbreak. By late October, hundreds of new cases were being reported each day, with 2,637 cases reported in the first month in Sacramento since the flu arrived.[104] The recently cleared Sacramento City Library on I Street was converted into Victory Hospital, schools and places of work closed and voters wore mandatory masks to the polls on election day. The Red Cross called for women and girls free from family duties to volunteer in efforts to stem the spread of the disease. For some, this meant leaving their jobs. By mid-November, fifty-seven nurses had joined, and they were overworked. They helped as auto drivers, ran diet kitchens and made 3,364 house calls, providing medical aid and housecleaning.[105] Some were paid, but many volunteered.

Prior to World War I, the only positions in the military deemed acceptable for women involved nursing the sick and wounded. Full mobilization now meant that employers would have to be more open-minded. Secretary of the navy Josephus Daniels challenged the exclusion of women from clerical work in his branch: "Is there any regulation which specifies that a Navy yeoman must be a man?"[106] Women soon after enlisted in the navy as yeomen in vital noncombatant roles, usually clerical. They also enlisted to work in wireless and first aid. Two of Sacramento's "yeomanettes" were Jessica E. Mott and Emma M. Doebler, who were stationed at Mare Island and the only women chosen among ten yeomen named from the Twelfth Naval District for transfer to Navy Department offices in Washington, D.C.[107]

Yeoman Lillie Catherine Todhunter, a young Sacramentan who worked for Phoenix Milling Company before the war, also served in the U.S. Naval Reserve at Mare Island. Todhunter graduated from Sacramento High School with the commercial class in June 1917. Her senior quote read, "A timid grace sits trembling in her eye." Todhunter enlisted in late August 1918 and tragically was a casualty of the Spanish influenza epidemic, the first woman in the history of the United States Navy to die while in active service. She received a full military funeral at Mather Field in Sacramento and was buried at St. Joseph's Cemetery.

Sacramento holds another unfortunate distinction in women's war service. The first American YMCA worker to be killed in the line of battle departed for the western front from this city. Marion Crandell, a forty-six-year-old tutor, left Sacramento for the western front to serve with the YMCA Canteen and was killed in action (struck by an enemy shell) at a French garrison near Verdun in March 1918. She taught French in Davenport, Iowa, and then at Ransome School in Berkeley before moving to Sacramento, where she was a tutor in the home of O.A. Robertson in the summer of 1917.[108]

Army nurse Julia E. Tesreau returned home to tell her story. She served "somewhere in France" for the Army Nurses' Corps with Base Hospital #30 for over a year. She wrote to the *Sacramento Bee* from New York in March 1918, on her way to France: "We will try to do for your boys—our boys—that which they have been deprived of—care, tenderness—and do our bit by soothing and giving assurance that we represent their loved ones at home."[109] When her letters to friends made their way into the *Bee* from her hospital in France that September, Tesreau gave a graphic and bleak picture of war in which "many and many a sad tale is told and lived and died."[110]

While women could join as nurses, the few women who were licensed doctors were barred from serving as such with the military. L. Etta Farmer, a medical doctor from Folsom, was district surgeon and a valued member of the community. When the war began, she organized the Red Cross chapter in that city and later went overseas to do relief work among the refugees

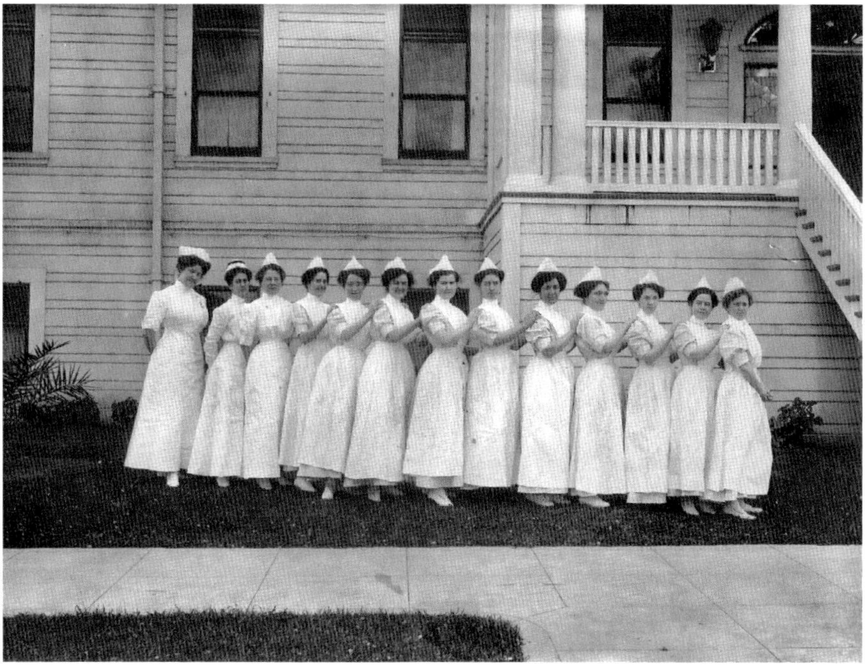

Nurses pose in front of White Hospital at the northeast corner of Twenty-ninth and J Streets, circa 1916. The hospital nursing school trained Red Cross and army nurses during the war. *Sacramento Public Library*.

in France. Other roles for women in the military included army telephone operators (for those who could speak French as fluently as English) and reconstruction aides recruited through the University of California Military Bureau. Reconstruction aides were needed in military hospitals overseas as nurse/teachers in occupational therapy after the war.

While women found war work in the home, community and abroad, they were blocked from the civilian labor force in jobs traditionally held by men until nearer the end of the war. Many gains in this area were pioneering, although limited in number. Where women did join the workforce, their strength and adaptability were a revelation to their co-workers.

The war brought the number of women in manufacturing in the United States from 1.4 million to somewhere around 1.5 million (in "essential war industries"), which was in line with increases during the prewar years. The greatest objections to using women related to the perceived threat of displacing men from useful work outside the home (and removing women from useful work inside the home) and the concern over whether women had the constitution for "real work." After the "work or fight" order of May 1918, men could not secure deferral of service if employed in occupations like clerk, elevator operator, waiter and doorman, causing a considerable number of women to shift into these positions. But America never mobilized women in the war industry to the extent that England and France did. The U.S. Department of Labor formed the Women in Industry Service (WIS) in August 1918, but the agency didn't make much progress prior to the end of the war. The practice at most places of employment was to upgrade men and in-fill with women, leading to few in skilled trades. Of those women who did find work in industrial positions, the majority were employed in "unskilled or semi-skilled processes of a repetitive nature," and the WIS downplayed the gains made by women during the war: "The various uniformed corps of society women and the bloomered munitions worker have had a somewhat romantic appeal to the public mind; but just how much this appeal will have accomplished toward securing equal opportunity and a square deal for working women is a matter of doubt."[111]

Wages for men and women were intended to be equal, but this wasn't always enforced. According to the National War Labor Board, women needed equal pay for three reasons: because "abstract justice" required that "payment be made according to service"; in order to keep up her family's standard of living; and to serve as a check on employment numbers by making women

A woman employed at Liberty Iron Works stands next to a Curtiss JN-4 (Jenny) plane. Women worked as stenographers, clerks and canvas sewers at the company. *Center for Sacramento History*.

no cheaper to hire than men. While the federal government communicated a commitment to equality—"Equal suffrage in industry is axiomatic with the National War Labor Board"[112]—local employers sometimes looked for ways to circumvent the law. Enforcement of the minimum wage was lacking in Sacramento fruit-packing plants according to a series of complaints filed with the deputy of the State Welfare Committee, John S. Blair. One girl was said to have been paid five cents for three days of work (the minimum was sixteen cents per hour).[113]

Women were peppered into manufacturing positions in the Sacramento area. They took up jobs in which their help was necessary due to a labor shortage. The Southern Pacific rail yard in Sacramento employed women for the first time in its history in August 1917.[114] The number of women employed nationally by the railroads picked up such momentum that by the end of the war, 50 percent of general office employees were women. The vast majority took clerical jobs. Southern Pacific women were hired to sort scrap iron and paid the same wages as men while the men shifted to heavier work. The women did "necessary, but non-critical" tasks considered suited to women—those that were repetitive and required precision. Women also took jobs in clerical and secretarial areas and worked in Pattern and Upholstery shops. Some kept these jobs following the war.[115]

In support of female war workers, the Young Women's Christian Association (YWCA) provided housing and recreation, along with education. In Sacramento, the club converted a "fine old mansion" at 1131 L Street into new quarters with parlors and cozy, comfortable reading rooms. In addition to offering courses in lighter fare like china painting, it directed women, ages nineteen to twenty-five, to a course in telegraphy that Western Union Telegraph offered at the Forum building.[116] The classes were offered for free due to government demand.

Positions that were traditionally filled by women felt a labor shortage due to the war and the Spanish influenza epidemic. A growing paucity of telephone operators led the Pacific Telephone & Telegraph Company to post ads in the *Sacramento Union* in October 1918 asking for more female applicants and requesting that residents use the phone only when necessary. Women forged entirely new paths in government and private-sector jobs to support their families. H.B. Christ was a pioneer auto saleswoman in Sacramento, "taking up the duties of being the head of the family while the husband [was] at the front fighting for the country." She sold Briscoes for I. Christie Motor Car Company and considered her occupation to be one of the best fields for women.[117] Mrs. W.W. Thomas and Mrs. Lida Bowman made use of connections in their small towns and were elected to office as justices of the peace in Orland and Galt. Mrs. Bowman did her best to communicate the value of a woman's work while downplaying its threat to the home. The *Sacramento Bee* reported that she was "not a feminist, neither does she believe in women neglecting her home, but she is a firm believer that a woman can do good in uplifting the politics of a small town."[118]

Perhaps the most expansive employment of women in men's jobs was through the Women's Land Army (WLA). Farms waited until the summer of 1918 to employ women, despite a serious labor shortage that had been evident since the previous spring. Women would be assigned to work a farm only after the state's Farm Labor Agent determined the need. WLA workers were paid twenty-five cents an hour (or the going rate, if higher), worked eight-hour days, got breaks every four hours and had Sundays off. As with other occupations, women who worked in the Women's Land Army distinguished themselves as quality workers. Miss Elsie Reed, a member of the WLA, took first prize in the tractor competition at a gathering of farmers in Davis in June 1918, "thus demonstrating the effectiveness of women in this line of endeavor."[119] Reed was one of three female tractor demonstrators employed by the Yuba Manufacturing Company. She graduated from the University of California–Berkeley and gave farm demonstrations on the University Farm in Davis. After a short course on tractors, she headed to Marysville, where she was put on the payroll as a machinist's helper. "Her advent into the shops, garbed in overalls and a soft hat, caused a stir among the men, but by asking no favors and doing her daily tasks with enthusiasm, intelligence and ability, she was soon accepted as an equal, and she did a man's work for a man's pay."[120]

Throughout the war, women were asked to serve primarily in the home. In addition to practicing conservation, they were in charge of moral reform and child welfare. In her talk "Women and the War" given at the Tuesday Club House in late October 1917, Mills College president Dr. Aurelia Henry Reinhardt stated that women would contribute the most by practicing home economy and food conservation. Above all, she encouraged women to stay in the home, where they could be a reforming influence, since the moral and physical problems of the soldiers were not due to training but to conditions in the home and the "low moral standard" of the cities from which they came.

Child welfare, from education to labor protection, was also understood to be a woman's domain, and Sacramento mothers were charged with reducing infant mortality for the war effort. When the national Children's Bureau requested that a Children's Year be established in 1918, President

Woodrow Wilson responded that "next to the duty of doing everything possible for the soldiers at the front, there could be, it seems to me, no more patriotic duty than that of protecting the children who constitute one-third of our population."[121]

Children's Year began on April 6, 1918, the anniversary of the U.S. entry into World War I. Sacramento babies were examined en masse as part of the national child welfare campaign to "go over the top" in registration and save 100,000 babies in 1918. Posters warned that in England, "it is safer to be a soldier in France than a baby at home." Children's Year made its way into the State Fair as well. Mothers responded to thirty questions on the proper care of babies in the Better Mothers Contest. Mrs. Frederick Bertram Wood of North Sacramento, mother of Frederick Bertram Wood Jr., won first prize in the contest at the 1918 fair. She took home a fifty-dollar Liberty Bond for "rearing him to strict scientific principles."[122]

In addition to running a household and raising healthy children, women were traditionally regarded as the moral guardians of the community. They provided good, clean fun for soldiers stationed at Mather Field through the War Camp Community Service, which formed out of the Playground and Recreation Association of America in order to combat venereal disease, which had ravaged troops during the Spanish-American War. The committee was to aid women in fashioning a "magic garment" of armor to protect soldiers wherever they may go and provide wholesome diversion to young soldiers, directing them to entertainment, churches, soldiers' clubs and home dinners in the community. The club also brought soldiers and girls together under "good influences."[123] In Sacramento, the organization set up a Sacramento Soldiers' and Sailors' Club at 727 J Street, with a well-stocked canteen, pool room and library. Run by "devoted and unselfish women," the club enjoyed more than two hundred visitors on a busy Sunday.[124] Local women with the War Camp Community Service Auto Recreation Corps would give sightseeing tours of the city and surrounding area to convalescent soldiers at Mather Field and provide transportation when needed. Governor Hiram W. Johnson declared women "not only a great reservoir of moral energy, but also a progressive force" while giving a talk on women's suffrage at a meeting of the Women's Council on January 21, 1914.[125] The Women's Council adopted resolutions sent to Congress suggesting legislation for prohibition and enforcement of ordinances regarding prostitution, gambling and the sale of intoxicating liquors in dance halls. They were to be a "precaution and protection" of the health of the combat forces stationed near Sacramento at the Army Aviation School at Mather Field. By tying drinking to larger wartime concerns, both as a corrupting vice for soldiers and as a drain on agricultural resources, women's groups supporting prohibition made advances during the war. "Win the War First, Then Prohibition" was the slogan for delegates at the Woman's Christian Temperance Union (WCTU) conference in Washington, D.C., and they established an intensive campaign for Prohibition in California to aid ratification of the national amendment.

Suffragists, who had significant overlap with Prohibitionists, also made gains. The Susan B. Anthony resolution for nationwide women's suffrage made its way to the Senate, where legislators were urged to adopt it as a war measure in December 1917. California women, who had been enfranchised since 1911, won the right to serve on juries in 1917. Sacramento senator J.M. Inman voted in the affirmative in opposition to J.W. Ballard of Los Angeles, who declared that "their habits, occupations and physiques do not fit them for jury duty."[126]

Just two days before the armistice, the Central Federated Union approved a report on reconstruction that asserted that "the same patriotism which induced women to enter industry during the war should induce them to vacate their positions after the war to make room for returned soldiers."[127] The small inroads that women made into the workforce during the war years were largely ceded back to returning soldiers. But the American woman would not "submit the habit of service to her country."[128] When the next world war hit, Sacramento and the rest of the nation recognized that women would be integral once again in winning the war.

5

THE WAR AND THE SCHOOL

By Amanda G. DeWilde

"Our country is at war. New duties and new tasks may be assigned to you, not too many and not too hard. You can help if you will. Your teacher will show you how. I have confidence in the patriotism of the boys and girls of California," Governor William D. Stephens appealed to the young people of California in the May 1917 pamphlet *All for America: What California Schools Can Do in the Present Crisis*. The patriotism of the boys and girls of Sacramento was on full display during the war years. Local schools answered Stephens's appeal with vigor and dedicated themselves to producing loyal citizens through Americanization, directing classroom activities toward the war and expanding services outside the classroom to support community efforts. Area schoolchildren learned about the purpose of the war and gave practical help. They farmed, canned, sewed, tinkered, cobbled and cut; they sang, debated, marched and sold bonds. Some joined the hundreds of student cadets in the Sacramento area, preparing for service once they were of age. K-12 schools in Sacramento County marshaled 16,380 students in total—nearly 20 percent of the county population—for the cause. Out of the war came a hardy generation better equipped for big challenges to come: the Great Depression and another world war.

Charles Colfax Hughes served as superintendent of city schools from 1912 to 1942. In his piece on "The War and the School," found within the School Department's 1917–19 report, Hughes reflected on schools' ambitious new purpose:

> *The war called for men and women trained to think logically, trained to produce, trained in thrift, trained in courage, trained in high moral standards, trained for physical strength, trained in loyalty, in patriotism, trained in obedience and respect for authority, imbued with ideals of independence and equality, trained for the love of fellowmen, recognizing the brotherhood of man and social unity.*

Hughes wanted to redirect focus away from the "intellectual monstrosities" produced by schools before the war. He also wanted to tear down the separation between school and society, impressing on his pupils real knowledge and real experience to meet real duties outside of the classroom. This goal was echoed throughout the county. Sacramento schools saw a boost in all things practical and patriotic. Physical education was added to the state curriculum in 1917. With the Smith-Hughes Act that year, Congress supplied states with financial assistance for vocational and agricultural education, along with home economics. Courses in citizenship, United States history and, especially, Americanization found increasing importance.

Americanization, or instruction in American culture and values, was the primary mandate of schools at all levels during the war years. Pro-American (and anti-German) instruction was emphasized to an extent not seen in

Serious young pupils sit in class at McKinley School at Seventh and G Streets in 1914. *Sacramento Public Library.*

the next world war or at any time since. In his address on "California and the War," delivered at the State War Council in March 1918, Governor Stephens communicated the importance of patriotic instruction: "The first big business of the American school is Americanism. The message of the war must go home to the people, and the teacher is in position to arouse the latent patriotic sentiment of the community and to awaken the fathers and mothers to their responsibility in this war crisis."[129]

Americanization first involved purging schools of all things pro-German. German clubs were the first to go, followed by language teaching and any pro-German elements in textbooks. A German Glee Club had formed at Sacramento High School in 1910, led by teachers Mr. Steinbach and Mr. Clewe. The group sang "simple folk songs together with the national hymns, and selections from the German masterpieces."[130] By 1911, it had transformed into a general German cultural club called *Das Deutsche Kranzchen*, and it enjoyed increasing numbers for the next few years. With war on the horizon, however, it disbanded in 1914 and resumed only in 1926.

By 1918, German songs had been eliminated from music curriculums at the request of the State Board of Education because they might have been considered offensive to national ideals. The board suggested that they be replaced by the daily use of songs stimulating a "vigorous National spirit."[131] In the spring of 1918, the Board of Education ordered an investigation of American and European history textbooks to root out "pro-Germanism" and to locate text that might be offensive to countries allied to the United States during the war. They deputized city and county school boards to cooperate in the hunt. Their goal: "One hundred percent Americanism in the schools of California."[132] And they did manage to remove any hint of Germanism in state textbooks. In early August 1918, the picture entitled "A School in Germany" in the California State Series' Grammar Book One was ripped from the covers, and text on the opposite page was blotted out under orders from the State Board of Education.

Despite the fact that France and England continued to teach it during the war, German-language classes were suspended in Sacramento. Superintendent Hughes demanded that German-language textbooks be taken out of Sacramento schools because he suspected them of being full of pro-German propaganda. He asserted that they would need to be radically changed before the study could be resumed after the war. "What we do want is the American language, and when I say American I mean American," he said in August 1918. "We want a country of all Americans, and not strips of country where various languages are spoken."[133] Although some

SHS

The Flag to our Hearts so Dear.

When the sun's bright rays
Cheer the golden days,
And our hearts are full and free,
We all gaze with love
At the flag above,
With its song of liberty.

When to school we go
And the breezes blow,
And the stars and stripes are clear,
Then they welcome you
With their red white and blue,
The flag we love so dear.

When we take our part
With a good stout heart,
In the work we have to do,
We will feel with pride
Our best we've tried,
To honor our flag so true.

We will give three cheers
(And in all these years,
Our hearts will never lag),
We will all be there,
No matter where,
Just to greet our dear old flag.

May Hing, '17.
S.H.S

EDNA DICKSON

A poem from the June 1917 Sacramento High School yearbook. *Sacramento Public Library.*

administrators were vehemently opposed to German instruction, students disagreed. Senior wills in Sacramento High School's June 1918 yearbook reflect some of the conflict. An anonymous student, "M.E.," willed "two German text-books in my possession to Miss Herrick in hopes she will cherish them as much as I do," while Beatric Farnham willed her "knowledge of the German language to Kaiser Bill, that it may be wiped from existence with him."

In addition to removing pro-German instruction, students were educated in patriotism and the purpose of the war. The State Board of Education adopted a course on war citizenship in January 1918 with the following lessons: "How Germany Sought to Dominate the World," "How Europe Was Aroused against Germany," "How War Came to America" and "The Defeat of Germany." A second issue of war citizenship lessons included "Helping Uncle Sam Finance the War," with emphasis on conservation of food and materials.

War themes were prevalent in debate as well. The public speaking class at San Juan Union High School tackled the prompt: "Resolved, that the United States should enter the European War against Germany." By the next fall, students argued only about how they might contribute. When the University of California Extension Division formed a Junior Section of the Interscholastic Public Speaking League of California, students in grammar and intermediate schools argued the prompt: "What can the American Boy or Girl do to Help the United States Win the War?"[134] And Galt High School tackled the proposition: "That California Was Justified in Passing the Anti-Alien Land Law" in their junior versus senior class debates in the spring of 1918.

Americanization also involved overriding the foreign allegiances of immigrant students and instilling in them a patriotic loyalty to their new country. "The Americanization of the people in and of America" was the principal theme of resolutions passed by the Third District convention of the Federated Parent-Teachers' Association held in Washington (Yolo County) in late January 1918. The association adopted resolutions to do everything in its power to Americanize foreign residents and to "bring them and our own people back to a realization of true democratic ideals."[135]

Sacramento boasted a sizable foreign-born population at the time: 10,873 foreign born in the city of Sacramento in 1920 out of the total population of 65,908.[136] Many of these immigrants were schooled in Americanism through the Foreign Night School, held after hours at Sacramento High School. The State Commission of Immigration and Housing maintained three "alien" schools in Sacramento: at Fourth and Q Streets, Eighteenth and K Streets,

A class portrait shows diversity at Lincoln School, circa 1917. The primary school boasted students representing twenty-one different nationalities. *Sacramento Public Library*.

Sacramento High School and Oak Park. Only one hundred students were enrolled in the night schools in April 1917, though it was estimated that four thousand needed instruction to become citizens.[137] Sacramento's chamber of commerce even formed a committee on immigration and housing that resolved to work with the state body to persuade employers to use their influence to get their employees to attend the school. Alice Peter, chairman of the War League of the Foreign Night School at Sacramento High School, was joined by Miss Emma Winter in conducting a successful Americanization school in Jackson, California, during the summer months at the request of local businessmen, who claimed that 50 percent or more of foreign mining workers were unable even to sign their names.

Foreign-language schools that had been established for young immigrant students felt pressure during these years. Most Sacramento County schools were integrated, and it was compulsory for all races to attend the same schools. But many Japanese children, who made up the largest foreign-born contingent in the county, also attended private Japanese schools after hours. The majority of students in the Florin District were Japanese, but it was the only district in the nation where this was the case. The schools primarily offered language instruction but were viewed with suspicion. While only Isleton segregated students prior to the war (in 1910), in 1921, the state legislature amended the school law of California, allowing for the segregation of children of Chinese, Japanese or Mongolian parentage.[138]

Mrs. William Hyman and Mrs. Bert Schlesinger of the Sacramento Children's Year Committee looked for ways to retain foreign students in public schools. They wanted to develop alternatives for "followers of fruit"—the children of migrant laborers who started school as late as November and were out as early as February. California law required students ages eight to fifteen to attend school while in session, which they were unable to do. Hyman and Schlesinger tied it into the war effort, "We must—and we can—develop constructive patriotism." They asked for watchers in every community to keep an eye out for the exploitation of foreign children.[139]

While foreign-born men and children were indoctrinated with Americanism at work and in school, foreign-born mothers were reached through California's Home Teachers program. The program was established through the Home Teachers Act of 1915, passed by the State Commission on Housing Immigration. The act sent women into homes to Americanize foreign-born housewives and, in turn, their families. It was established with the understanding that the state would be unsafe when there was "no knowledge of its language or the ideas for which it stands" in a large number of its homes. The work of home teachers was "to work in the homes of the pupils, instructing children and adults in matters relating to school attendance and preparation, sanitation, in the English language, in household duties such as purchase, preparation and use of food and of clothing and in the fundamental principles of the American system of government and the rights and duties of citizenship." They were trained to establish a sympathetic, trusting connection and then begin to suggest improvements in the care of house and children, thereby having a "direct Americanizing influence." Home teachers were required to have a teaching certificate, fluency in the most prevalent language in their service district, empathy, good health, tact and patience, among other attributes. The commission published a manual of best practices for home teachers wherein it gave advice on spotting the ideal candidate: "Look for a woman who has the social instinct, with a personal approach which attracts, and invites confidence."[140]

In addition to her Foreign Night School work, home teacher Alice Peter instructed Sacramento women in the purchase, preparation and use of food and clothing. She also taught home sanitation, helped out with a city cleanup and reported cases where children were attending no school. Peter reported that thirty-nine county schools and eight city schools were attended by a considerable proportion of foreign students. Although originally an outgrowth of the war effort, home teachers continued their work in Sacramento homes after the war.

At the outset of war, there was some concern that the youth of California would need to be made aware of the reality of war (short of inciting hysteria) and that much propaganda was needed to motivate them to contribute. Area schools invited speakers to make the battle abroad more real. Madame Dupriez, wife of a Belgian visiting professor at Harvard, visited Sacramento High School to give a talk and raise funds for Belgium. Lord Dunmore, a British soldier, gave a talk to students on April 5, and Captain Sneddon from New Zealand shared stories about the Australian and New Zealand armies. An "enthusiastic" captain of the Italian army also visited with slides of the armies' operations in the Alps, and Mr. Titus of the local YMCA chapter showed "trophies" of the battlefield.[141]

Schools and their students demonstrated commitment to the war effort by directing their studies and activities toward helping the Allies. Reading, language and composition, spelling, arithmetic and other foundational subjects were tinged by war themes, as were applied studies like drawing, music and manual and physical training. The conservation of food through self-control and self-sacrifice was to be taught in schools at the proclamation of Governor Stephens. He ordered a regular period each Monday, beginning on January 7, 1918, to be devoted to instruction in how each child might aid the national food campaign.[142] In addition to food conservation, students cultivated land around their schools and on available public lands for war gardens.

The schools began to teach practical skills and aid the war effort through manual training departments for boys and domestic science departments for girls. Within their manual training departments, Sacramento schools constructed facilities for instruction in barbering, shoemaking, sewing, rug making, tinsmithing and canning. Students in these classes produced swab sticks and bedside tables, knitting needles and Red Cross folding tables. The manual training departments at the high school level added war-related instruction to prepare students for entry into the army or navy: radio-buzzer class for men preparing to enter the Army Signal Corps, automobile repair, camp carpentry, blacksmithing and military surveying and mapping.

In the domestic science department at Sacramento High School, Miss Weymouth worked at "rooting out the unessentials [*sic*], and combining in its course only the things of the most practical nature."[143] She supervised the conservation of food, with special days to accommodate learning from local housewives on canning fruit and vegetables. In the "spirit of thrift and a willingness to subordinate self for humanity and country,"[144] students taught

A patriotic school band in front of Marshall School at Twenty-seventh and G Streets, 1917. *Library of Congress.*

Students cobble shoes in a manual training class. Classes in vocational studies gained in popularity and funding during the war years. *Sacramento Public Library.*

High school students demonstrate potato cooking at Weinstock, Lubin & Co. store. *Center for Sacramento History.*

food conservation with a demonstration kitchen at the California State Fair and hosted potato demonstrations in Weinstock, Lubin & Co. stores. Their conservation recipes made it into the *Sacramento Bee* each week. The department set up a diet kitchen during the Spanish influenza epidemic near the end of the war and during the war sewed pieces and garments for the Junior Red Cross, Red Cross and French and Belgian Relief. Sewed pieces were in such demand that the Sewing Department turned into an auxiliary of the Red Cross, with girls reporting that they would rather do the work of the Red Cross than "make fancy things for themselves."[145] The girls at San Juan Union High School also formed a Red Cross unit with forty-eight domestic science students enlisted. They sewed under the supervision of Miss Marjorie Landers, working on surgical aprons and, later, fashioning complete surgical outfits.[146]

Students in the city schools produced all sorts of items for the war effort: 317 comfort pillows; 1,962 sweaters; 3,457 refugee garments; 23 canes; 254 helmets; and 132 infant kits. They wrote 3,044 essays for the Liberty Loan campaigns. Speeches for war occasions were given by 926 students. Students founded Victory Boys and Victory Girls clubs at Leland Stanford School and Bret Harte School.[147] They sent books and magazines to soldiers, and they purchased Liberty Bonds totaling $374,875 (or $27 per student) and War Savings and Thrift Stamps totaling $126,584 ($9 per student). Students did much to raise funds for the various campaigns. In June 1917, 5,000 schoolchildren were unleashed on the city under the supervision of their teachers to sell tags—money from which would go toward the National War Work Council. And in a grand parade in October 1917, 10,000 schoolchildren, kindergarten through high school, marched down J Street to raise subscriptions of Liberty Bonds, doing their part to "swell the voice of free America" by tugging at Sacramento's heart strings. They held banners reading, "Children Are Being Bombed in England" and "My Daddy Is Fighting for Your Liberty." The goal of the parade and bond drive was to help establish lasting peace for the marchers and "insure them against another dreadful war in future years."[148]

War-related instruction and activities extended into the community. Under the Civic Center Law, schools opened their facilities for adult education, citizenship classes, mothers' afternoon millinery and sewing classes and courses in cooking and canning war garden products. Classrooms also were made available for Red Cross training and work. When the Federal Board of Vocation Education called for evening classes in telegraphy, Sacramento High School sent out notices about new classes directed by night superintendent Frank Tade to drafted men interested in radio and buzzer telegraphy.[149] Schools also hosted community Liberty League meetings at Lincoln School, William Land School, Newton Booth School, Mary J. Watson School and Marshall School.

In their commitment to conservation, schools cut back on anything they deemed extravagant. There were no big social balls at Sacramento High School in the spring of 1918 because the school was asked to refrain from giving "costly parties or banquets" for the period of the war.[150] The school's 1918 Senior Dance benefited the Red Cross, as did the very popular Sophomore Fair, held at the school grounds. Fraternities and sororities also were deemed frivolous. On May 15, 1917, a protest against the fraternities and sororities existing in the local high schools under the guise of "clubs" was voiced by the Woman's Council. The council pledged to wipe out the clubs because they prevented city and county schools from building better citizens.[151] It was echoing commissioner Gus Turner's recent criticism of the "undemocratic and un-American" groups. Turner called them a waste of public funds: "These organizations are costing taxpayers money which they may as well pour down a rat-hole for all the good it does."[152]

While more controversial in other parts of the state, compulsory military drill and the establishment of a cadet corps were embraced in the Sacramento

Sacramento High School's cadet company officers, 1918. *Sacramento Public Library*.

area. The first provision for military training in California schools came through an act approved by the state legislature on April 5, 1911: "High Schools May Establish Military Companies." Cadet corps were to have a minimum of forty members, which excluded smaller schools from joining. In February 1916, there were sixteen companies statewide; in February 1917, there were thirty-five. In San Diego, Los Angeles and Oakland, teachers and parents challenged the establishment of military training in schools. The vast majority with cadet companies early on were Northern California schools. The cadet corps at Sacramento-area schools, including Sacramento High School (with a total enrollment of 1,171), Auburn High School (206 students) and Marysville High School (175 students), enjoyed robust numbers.

Sacramento High School established its cadet training, the Sacramento High School Cadet Corps, in February 1912. The corps grew from a company of 40 in 1912 to 235 cadets in four companies in 1918. The cadets built an indoor rifle range on the roof with money from the City of Sacramento, thanks to the work of commissioner of education E.J. Carragher. Cadets also participated in exercises within the school and at regional events. At annual exhibitions, the companies competed for best-drilled company, most rapid signaling, fastest wall scaling, the best-drilled cadet and the most accurate rifleman. Lieutenant Adolph Merwin wore the medal for best rifleman at the high school in 1918, making a score of ninety-six out of one hundred.[153]

The highlight of the cadet year was the annual encampment. Four hundred high school cadets encamped at Camp William D. Stephens at Del Paso Park for a five-day training in April 1918. Cadets hailed from Sacramento, Marysville, Auburn, Roseville, Stockton and Gridley. Under the command of Major Mallett of the Coast Artillery, the "jazziest and peppiest man that they had ever met," the cadets held sham battles; performed army maneuvers, bayonet practice and signal work; and listened to lectures. On their last day, they proudly paraded in front of Governor Stephens.[154] Military drill of up to one hour each day was made compulsory for junior and senior boys for the 1918–19 school year.

While girls were excluded from cadet corps, 55 Grass Valley High School girls set up their own military company and held drill at Columbus School, led by military school graduate Professor Hendershot.[155] More than 300 boys at the Preston School of Industry, a reform school in Ione, also wanted to be part of the action and volunteered their services for their country through president of the board A.M. Seymour in April 1917. They had already received military training, lacking only target practice.[156] In 1918, 25 students were bused to Fort McDowell on Angel Island to entrain under the command of a recruiting officer, Sergeant Elrod. Though 23 wished to enlist in the aviation corps, all were rejected because of "commitments" and returned home, excepting three boys who ran away. However, 148 Preston boys did enlist in the army and navy during the war.[157]

In August 1918, the navy and Navy Reserve Recruiting Station at Ninth and K Streets received word from the secretary of the navy that young men under draft age were urged to continue their studies in high school or college rather than enlist.[158] While enrollment in college did not disqualify one from being drafted, there was a way for men to remain in school during the war. Most high school graduates in Sacramento who would have otherwise gone on to junior college or other vocational training were encouraged to enter the Student Army Training Corps after graduation. The corps trained male students who had registered for the draft and commissioned them into active duty. The student soldiers remained in school and were offered vocational and collegiate sections. Instruction was modified to serve army needs "along lines of direct military value," with coursework in subjects like medicine, engineering and chemistry, but the schools paid for housing, subsistence and instruction. Host colleges like the University of California–Berkeley were asked to direct their whole energy and educational power toward training corps students according to military dictates.[159]

Because Sacramento men enrolled in Student Army Training Corps programs throughout the state, none was permitted to register at the new Sacramento Junior College for the fall of 1918. Sacramento Junior College began as a department of Sacramento High School on the upper floor of the school at Eighteenth and K Streets. It was intended, like other California junior colleges, as "terminal work for the great mass of high school graduates, who can not, will not and should not become university students."[160] The school opened with forty-six students, but its development was stunted by the war. In addition to the loss of male students to the Army Training Corps, more women were entering the workforce. Consequently, the junior college stagnated in 1917 and closed for the 1918–19 school year. Its first class graduated six students in June 1918—all women who planned to continue on to university. Belle Cooledge, who later went on to become the first female mayor in Sacramento, reopened the school in 1920 in its own wing at the new Sacramento High School at Thirty-fourth and Y. She served as dean for many years prior to her entry into politics.

Belle Cooledge (left) took a sabbatical from Sacramento Junior College to serve as a nurse for the army during the war. *Sacramento Public Library*.

Like many other teachers and administrators, Belle Cooledge took a sabbatical during the war to work as a nurse for the army.[161] H.O. Williams, principal of Sacramento High School, also took a year's leave of absence to engage in war work. Because war work was more popular and teaching was not a vocation recognized for general exemption from military service, the profession experienced a labor shortage. Older teachers were called back into the service, and newly married women fought to keep their jobs. As had been tradition, schools continued the policy of firing female teachers once they married with the justification that they no longer needed the salary and would not be able to effectively manage both roles. E.R. Snyder of the Commission of Vocational Education had opposed the practice of letting married teachers go and now called on schools to retain married women as a wartime necessity. When Miss Edith McNie became Mrs. Edith McNie Davis and feared losing her job, D.W. Carmichael took steps to revisit (and repeal) the rule adopted by the Sacramento Board of Education. Superintendent Hughes, however, argued against the change, saying that it would lead to a sociological problem, as married teachers would have divided minds.[162]

Teachers in Sacramento County already had a great deal of responsibility before the war, as the majority of the Sacramento County schools were rural and decentralized. Although a few dozen schools served city students, the bulk were educated in one- and two-room schoolhouses organized into seventy-five small districts throughout the county. Schools had been expanding into agricultural suburbs but remained in fragmented districts. New school districts included Robla School District (1917), North Sacramento School District (1914), American Basin School (1916), Rio Linda School District (1917) and Jefferson School District (1918). When educators explored the possibility of centralizing the California school systems, a minority declared that it had as its object "the development of pupils who are mere machines of efficiency—in other words, it would Prussianize the schools."[163]

Demands on teachers and criticism of their work increased during the war years—they were expected to lead students in war work and, perhaps more importantly, instill patriotism. To direct their own war work, area teachers formed the Sacramento Teachers' War Service League. Officers were to serve the local Liberty Loan Committee, Thrift Stamp Committee, Food Administration, Exemption Boards, Council of Defense and Red Cross. They did many things, including clerical work, soliciting and distributing, public speaking, working with the Red Cross, teaching languages, craft work and directing boys in farm work.[164] When 1,500 teachers met at the Northern California Teachers' Association conference in Sacramento, from October 30 through 31, 1917, their theme was "service." Discussion topics revolved around food conservation and instruction in loyalty and patriotism.

Teachers were to fan the flames of loyalty and patriotism in their students while modeling both of these ideals to "consecrate [themselves] to the duty of arousing the people."[165] Their success toward this goal was closely followed by the boards of education and other loyalty groups. The California Loyal League, formed in January 1918, had the motto, "Stand by the Government," and its mission was to "stamp out treason in the California public schools and show up the teachers who are disloyal."[166] The group requested that all California teachers sign an oath of allegiance or resign. They made President Woodrow Wilson honorary chairman.

Teachers who didn't fall in line faced censure. At Sacramento High School, teachers were investigated for failing to encourage students to assist in the government's harvesting plans over the summer. Instead, they were accused of signing up students for private night classes and charging them fifty cents per head per hour. School was to be postponed until later in the fall so that students could help out with farm labor, but this arrangement ended when Sacramento High School principal H.O. Williams argued that students helping with the harvest lived outside the city school district.[167]

In November 1917, twelve teachers were called on by the City Board of Education to explain why they didn't march in the recent Liberty Loan Parade. Some gave physical excuses, and others protested due to conscience or modesty. Teacher Henrietta Adroit stood before the board and said, "I want to make a protest against exploiting the schools for any purpose. If we want to be patriotic we want to keep our hands off the public schools. We want the schools to turn out educated children. Too much time is lost with parades and things of that nature."[168] Miss Caroline Stevenson also infuriated the school board by asserting that it had no authority over her as far as religion and conscience. At least a couple of other women thought it unbecoming to march in a parade.

Upon passage of the Sedition Act the following spring, those teachers would have risked harsher punishment. Myra Dunton, a Lodi teacher and socialist, served a term of forty days in the Sacramento County jail on a charge of disloyalty beginning in late June 1918 and was barred from ever again teaching in public schools in California at the insistence of state superintendent of public instruction Edward Hyatt. Hyatt stated that no teacher should retain her certificate once convicted of "pro-Germanism."[169] Dunton had allegedly remarked that she "could not teach in a school over which that dirty rag floated," referring to the U.S. flag.[170] She had been teaching for more than ten years and earned her certificate from the San Jose Normal School. After her release, she went on to run a dairy farm in Lake County's Bachelor Valley.

With determined patriotism, Sacramento schools put their full force into the war effort and emerged on the other side transformed. In his 1919 report on city schools, Hughes stated that the schools had been "revitalized through an intense motive." He feared the disunity and slow of progress that the postwar years might bring. But Sacramento's teachers and students would continue their tradition of service. During the Spanish influenza epidemic near the end of the war, 159 teachers worked with the Red Cross, and 111 of them served as nurses. They cooked in the city's diet kitchen, did clerical work, made masks and did laundry for sick families. Just after the war, schools joined in unified districts, junior high schools were created and the Sacramento Junior College found new life. The war made the Sacramento school work smarter and more efficiently; as Hughes reflected, the war "socialized it, it motivated it, made it more closely related to life, made it a real education."[171]

6

COLUMBIA IS A JEALOUS MOTHER

By James C. Scott

It was the morning of April 18, 1917, and nine-year-old Henry Gutenberger had spring fever. From his home at 3131 Y Street, he dawdled through the morning sun, book strap slung over his shoulder, maintaining just enough compass to push himself in a southeasterly direction toward Bret Harte Primary School at Fourth Avenue and Sacramento Boulevard. It was also Wednesday, which meant that he was a bit closer to the weekend and a trip to his beloved midway at Joyland. As Henry turned onto Thirty-sixth Street, two familiar faces—more acquaintances than friends—stood shoulder-to-shoulder, arms folded, blocking the entrance to the school's play yard. And then it started. "HUN-ry!"—"Hohenzollern!"—"Guten Tag, Kaiser Hank!" One of the boys made a grab for Henry's books while the other pushed him to the ground. It was somewhere amid the tears that started to stream down his cheeks that he realized why all of this was happening.

The day prior, Henry had refused to wear a small American flag that his teacher placed on the chest of every student in her class. Although his mother and father were American born, his grandmother was a native of Germany and, according to Henry, would beat him if he came home wearing the flag. The boy's mother, Gertrude, expressed surprise at the incident, stating that she was going "to talk to the boy about it," and "as far as wearing the flag is concerned…[she was]…not opposed to it."[172] Regardless of where the truth lay, the frayed Gutenbergers made sure that an American flag was flying from their front porch the next morning.

The vignette of Henry Gutenberger was far from rare. America's entry into the Great War placed its ethnic Germans under the watchful eye of every level of government, a cabal of semi-governmental vigilance groups, the general public and even little boys from Oak Park. In this frenzy to stamp out "pro-Germanism," millions of Americans, in the words of historian Daniel Farber, "spied on neighbors, eavesdropped on suspicious conversations in bars and restaurants, intercepted the mail and telegrams of suspected dissidents, and reported to authorities any evidence of disenchantment with the war effort."[173] Pacifists, socialists, suffragists, labor reformers, those with no interest (or perceived to have no interest) in the war effort, those who spoke out against it and even those who misspoke fell into the mix of judgment as well. Of all these groups, immigrants did the heaviest lifting—Irish and East Indians because of their antipathy toward England and Jews by way of their hostility toward an anti-Semitic Russian government. But as we will see, it was the nation's ethnic Germans—carrying both the blood and custom of a hated enemy—who bore the brunt of Anglo-American animus.

Germanic origins in the Sacramento Valley can be traced back to two mid-century migratory events: the gold rush and the European revolutions of 1848. As with other culture groups, California offered Germans a blank canvas for self-reinvention; they could acculturate to the ways of a new land but also carry over their most cherished ethnic traditions. In time, names like Breuner, Heilbron, Dreher, Teichert, Meister and Ruhstaller (German Swiss) distinguished themselves as leaders in regional business, politics and society. They were respected community members who paid into the tax base, paraded with the Turnverein on Independence Day and freely gave themselves and their children to military service. They also valued public education. If American political philosophy assumed that the democratic process could not survive without a literate citizenry, ethnic Germans had more than done their bit. In the first decade of the twentieth century, the group's illiteracy rate sat at 5.1 percent, compared to 26.7 percent for all other immigrant groups.[174]

Sacramento proper, as seen through the 1920 census, offers a telling sample of the region's Teutonic footprint. Out of a total city population of 65,908, 16 percent—or 10,873—were foreign born. Within that foreign-born figure, one-quarter came from a Central Power nation, the bulk being German, at 1,198. The city's second-generation German Americans, having had at least one parent born in Germany, numbered 4,380, or 7 percent of the city's total population. By 1920, then, 8.8 percent of Sacramentans were either born in Germany or had at least one parent who was. Throwing Austria into the mix pushes that percentage up to nearly 10 percent.

However, a string of diplomatic crises—the sinking of the *Lusitania* in 1915, the interception of the Zimmerman Telegram in 1917 and the resumption of unrestricted submarine warfare, also in 1917—pushed the region's old-stock Anglo-Americans to look at their Germanic neighbors with an increasingly skeptical eye. And yet it also seemed reasonable to most German Americans that statements and gestures of solidarity would allay most fears of disloyalty. The San Joaquin County German Aid Society eagerly adopted a resolution expressing that "every member…openly avows…loyalty to the government of the United States, first, secondly, and for all time."[175] Farther up the valley and not a week after the declaration of war, Austrian Americans Mateo Lopisich and James Rudech offered a sixty-acre tract of land at Fifth Avenue and Sixtieth Street to Sacramento's city commission for a military training camp. In July, Marysville's German Social Club, made up mainly of ethnic Germans from both Sutter and Yuba Counties, gave

German-born Henry Schaefer's 915 K Street Bakery. He vowed to pay the Red Cross $5,000 if anyone could prove him to be un-American. *Center for Sacramento History.*

a benefit for the American Red Cross. And in August, Sacramento's A.E. Meister and Sons, a well-regarded, German American–owned carriage and automobile manufacturing concern, sought to surrender its Alkali Flat plant to the War Department for the purpose of building airplane parts. Although commonplace throughout the valley, the impact of these and similar gestures proved minimal.

Within days after the declaration of war, large private interests like the Southern Pacific Railroad and Pacific Gas and Electric feared sabotage to the point of posting armed guards at bridges, dams, power stations and strategic rights of way. SP sent 150 men to various locations throughout its Sacramento Division, which stretched from Sacramento to Sparks, Nevada. Equally concerned, the State Highway Division placed private guards at several of its bridges, as well as at the newly constructed Yolo Causeway. The division's first arrest was made in mid-April on the Yuba River, near Marysville. The offender was a man named L. Desere. Guards thought that the furtive Frenchman was transporting dynamite, but as was quickly discovered, he was simply trying to conceal an eight-and-a-half-pound Plymouth Rock chicken that he had just stolen from a local farm. Within Sacramento County, so-called Home Guard units—ad hoc assemblages composed mainly of men too old for the draft—took up arms for community defense against German saboteurs, the IWW and others. Roughly 250 men made up companies drawn from Oak Park, North Sacramento and Sacramento proper. Oak Park's Home Guard, known officially as the Twenty-sixth Company, had 65 members who included jeweler Josiah Babcock as the oldest, at fifty-six, and policeman Ralph Towns as the youngest, at twenty-six. Without uniforms and without military issue weapons, they held nighttime drills in spots that included nearby Joyland, the no-man's-land section lying between Sacramento proper and North Sacramento, and the Capital City rifle range. One late September evening in 1917 in North Sacramento, a driver became so alarmed at the sight of the motley, wood gun–carrying Home Guards out on maneuvers, that he, in the words of one trooper, "stepped on 'er," escaping the spot at nearly sixty miles per hour.[176] Just minutes later, the same group was attacked by a watchdog.

Humor aside, the nation's public and private interests had some reason for concern. Although not great in number, there were pro-German Americans who were willing to do their part to effect a positive outcome for the Central Powers. By the end of 1915, thirty-seven munitions factory explosions had occurred across the country, and although there was no physical evidence to link them to a pro-German element, the sheer numbers were concerning enough. The proof finally came when munitions plants at Black Tom Island, New Jersey (July 1916); Kingsland, New York (January 1917); and Mare Island, California (March 1917), were indeed razed by German saboteurs. The popular press—including spy-hunting "experts" like newspaperman/detective Max Cook—was off and running, obliging an increasingly harried Anglo-American readership with gaudy reports of a rising shadow nation of Hohenzollern spies. In the spring of 1918, Cook, the city editor for the *St. Louis Republic*, syndicated with papers throughout the country, including the *Sacramento Star*, a six-part citizen primer on spy catching. Cook's first installment launched with the cheap tease, "Your Neighbor, Your Maid, Your Lawyer, Your Waiter, May be a German Spy."[177] Now given ample reason to be frightened, hundreds of thousands of Americans sought to organize and fight back.

In 1917, the Bureau of Investigation, while fully engaged in domestic counterespionage, had just four hundred special agents and a support staff of three hundred to cover the entire nation. This forced the agency to dip into an American citizenry that was primed to help. Much in line with the age-old precepts of Anglo-American common law that demanded male citizens be the defenders of their immediate community, a patchwork of "treason leagues" emerged across the nation. The West Coast–centered Nathan Hale Volunteers, who went public as early as April 6, were described as a "secret interstate citizens intelligence organization," whose operatives—working under the safety of anonymity—would "aid the government in connection with anti-spy, pro-German and anti-American activities."[178] The higher-profile American Protective League (APL), founded in February 1917 and described by historian David Kennedy as a "band of amateur sleuths and loyalty enforcers," set up its Northern California headquarters in San Francisco with chapters, most notably, in Sacramento and Elk Grove.[179] Other organizations smattered about the country, their names truly defying belief, included the Sedition Slammers, the Terrible Threateners and the Boy Spies of America.[180]

The group with the most Sacramento traction was the Liberty League (LL), which, coming into its prime in the spring of 1918, had chapters throughout the city in spots like North Sacramento, Elmhurst, Watson School, Marshall School, Highland Park, Oak Park, Riverside and Curtis Oaks. Spearheading their establishment was Sacramento County Defense Council chairman Judge Peter Shields, who felt that smaller, neighborhood-based chapters, as opposed to a single countywide organization, would be more efficient "in stamping out disloyalty and promoting patriotism."[181] In addition to the

Defense Council, the Justice Department, Bureau of Investigation and U.S. Army would all claim some hand in underwriting the very presence of the LL, not to mention the APL. And despite the Justice Department making it clear that the groups carried no legal authority, overenthusiastic members felt as if they had been deputized, in effect licensed to aggressively flash their shiny badges about and act with an entitlement seldom seen before (or since) in American war-making. And yet, one of the great strains of moral tension emanating from Great War America involved these super-patriotic groups. Defending the nation in its hour of need, they found themselves, often unwittingly, violating the civil liberties of thousands of innocents, both citizens and non-citizens, who paradoxically stood as the very people the LL and APL had sworn to protect, epitomizing, in the words of historian Michael Sulick, "the dangers of efforts to pursue spies and saboteurs unsupported by law and precisely defined authorities."[182] It was at these ultra-local jurisdictions, overseen by county Defense Councils and so distant from the halls of the Justice Department, where the worst oppression of Americans took place.[183]

Beating the drum for such groups was George Creel's Committee on Public Information (CPI), or what amounted to a tax-subsidized public relations firm charged with selling the war to the American people and portraying the nation's enemies in the worst possible light. Creel's background as businessman, muckraking journalist and police administrator made him a seamless match for the CPI; he knew people, he knew organizational structure, he knew the law and he knew how to sell a cause. Through a colorful mélange of posters, a seventy-five-thousand-person army of persuasive orators (known as "four-minute men") and films, the CPI's ability to mold public sentiment was revolutionary and the standard by which future wars, particularly World War II, would be promoted by the U.S government. As for Sacramento, the CPI contributed to some of the American West's most attractive window merchandising. Weinstock's display manager Charles Morton won national recognition for both himself and his employer through a series of CPI-funded window displays that encouraged Sacramentans to dislike the Kaiser, contribute to bond drives, conserve resources and enlist in the military.

The Weinstock's/CPI collaboration was a sincere relationship based on encouragement and counsel. However, it was the CPI that also gave particular attention to the nation's ethnic Germans in a way that "abetted the oppression of innocent citizens as it agitated against an imagined German spy system," eventually cultivating a public "hatred for anything German."[184] A local

This 1918 photograph captures one of Weinstock, Lubin's award-winning window displays. The Committee on Public Information helped. *Center for Sacramento History.*

example of this came from James W. Gerard, former American ambassador to Germany, and his promotion of *My Four Years in Germany*, a chronological exposé of the diplomat's time in Berlin. The book's film adaptation was advertised in local newspapers as the "Greatest Film of All Times—Not Fiction, But the Truth!" complete with garish spreads of helmeted gorillas carrying clubs in one hand and French babies in the other. The flick played to packed houses at K Street's Strand Theater for the last week of May 1918. Gerard's political and diplomatic cache, the CPI's endorsement of the movie and an overwrought script full of dachshunds, pointy helmets and sinister mustachios simply fed the Capital City's already frothed anti-German tenor. To provide some sense of his anti-German vitriol, Gerard, in a speech given just after the war, recounted a conversation between himself and Germany's foreign minister, Theobald von Bethmann-Hollweg:

> *The Foreign Minister of Germany once said to me your country does not dare do anything against Germany, because we have in your country*

My Four Years in Germany played at Sacramento's Strand Theater and was authorized by the Committee on Public Information. *Sacramento Public Library.*

> *five hundred thousand German reservists who will rise against your government if you dare to make a move against Germany. Well, I told him that that might be so, but that we have five hundred thousand and one lamp posts in this country, and that that was where the reservists would be hanging the day after they tried to rise.*[185]

Between eye-popping, educational window displays and abetting scorched-earth personalities like Gerard's, the CPI was a curious straddler of two poles of action: one as educator of responsible civil behavior during wartime and one as accelerant to the madness driving the fanaticism of groups like the APL and LL. Of course, independent of the CPI, media reports did their part in recruiting members to the treason leagues. This included tales of mysterious wireless apparatuses being found along Sacramento's Thirteenth Street, a supposed German suitcase bomb found in Butte County (which turned out to be a suitcase full of clothing and powder puffs) and a dead serviceman who was poisoned in an I Street saloon by a man who "appeared" to be German.

It is also true that one could be of Anglo-American heritage and still incur the wrath of the LL, as Isaac Peterson found out in April 1918. The proprietor of a hotel on Auburn Boulevard, Peterson was investigated by the

Judge Peter Shields was in charge of Sacramento County's Council for Defense and built Liberty League chapters to hunt down the disloyal. *Sacramento Public Library.*

LL's North Sacramento Chapter for supposedly calling Liberty Bonds a "damned graft" while in conversation with a local justice of the peace.[186] For his comment, Peterson was made to stand before the league's ruling council—not to mention a hostile crowd of one hundred LL members—for deposition. Peterson simply said that he had no more money to give to the war effort and that his comments were more so directed at the possibility of graft within the bond drive program. He went on to say, "I'd like to put a rope around the Kaiser's neck and drag him through the streets."[187] A subsequent league investigation found that Peterson, in its eyes, had ample funds to purchase bonds, as he owned a four-hundred-acre ranch in South Dakota, as well as an automobile. As punishment, he suffered the indignity, by way of chapter vote, of never being able to become a member of the LL, was forced to purchase a $100 bond and had his case referred to Martin Welsh, commissioner of the United States District Court for the Northern District of California.

Not every LL case was referred to federal authorities for prosecution under the Espionage and Sedition Acts. However, within the month of May 1918, 30 from around the region were sent Welsh's way. Cases of note included alleged pro-German comments made by Buffalo Brewery bottler Carl Schilter; George Fleming for threatening to shove the German flag down the throat of Sacramento Brave baseball player Paul Horil for denunciating the kaiser; and Arbuckle's Dora Porter, a naturalized American citizen from Germany, for saying that she "hoped every boy in Camp Lewis would be drowned on his way across the Atlantic or else killed over there."[188] In the end, the wartime weight of federal law fell on roughly 2,200 Americans, although just 1,055 of them were actually convicted, and of the latter, a great majority was pardoned, the most notable being Socialist leader Eugene V. Debs. Schilter, Fleming and Porter were never convicted for their statements.

It is also true that whatever it took for an ethnic German to measure up to the standards of full Americanism could often be a moving target, within view in the fall but perhaps not so much in the spring. Sixty miles south of Sacramento, the city of Tracy was home to a robust population of hundreds of German Americans who found work through the railroad, the operation of small businesses and a burgeoning agricultural industry. They worked hard and found relaxation and outlet through Tracy's saloons, card-gaming, church-driven social activities and ethnic-centered groups like the Ladies German Club. Yet once the war was underway and Tracy's own chapter of the Liberty League exerted itself, German Americans shed themselves of anything that might make them seem less American. Language, perhaps the most visible manifestation of culture, was the first to go. Subscriptions to the *German Demokrat*, a San Francisco–published German-language newspaper, were cancelled, and visits into Tracy proper for social outings became fewer and fewer.

By October 1918, German-born harness maker Gustave August Daniel Buschke felt like he had done his part for victory. His sons, Clinton and Oscar, both registered for the draft (the former serving as a U.S. Marine); he purchased war bonds; and he gave to the American Red Cross. However, by the time of the Fourth Liberty Bond Drive, Buschke was strapped to the point of exasperation, as expressed in the following slip: "If I were stood up to the wall and shot, I could not and would not buy one."[189] Not long after Buschke's comment, he was visited by two policemen and paraded into downtown Tracy by torchlight. Once there, he was forced to kiss the American flag and then made to watch his business and home painted yellow, the handiwork of the local LL's so-called decoration committee.[190] Across the country, the yellow washing of property was a somewhat customary practice for punishing those community members who were deemed disloyal. A statue of Johann Wolfgang von Goethe in Chicago's Lincoln Park was also painted yellow, as were hundreds of German churches nationwide.

Where the net of the LL and APL could not reach, flash mobs often could. In April 1917, Adolph Langfelder, a San Francisco cabinetmaker and native of Austria, was in charge of a work crew at Grass Valley's Nevada County Bank Building. When news appeared of the Eddystone, Pennsylvania munitions plant explosion—one that killed sixty people—Langfelder remarked, "They ought to be blown up; that's the only way—blow 'em all up."[191] With the comment traveling quickly about town, Langfelder encountered a crowd waiting outside his hotel that immediately threw him to the ground, forcing him to flee to his worksite for safety. By that evening, the group had decided to dispatch Langfelder from town, but not before making him kiss the American flag and then carry it through downtown Grass Valley. After doing so, he caught the first train back to San Francisco. There is also the curious death of John Deus, an ethnic German living in the now-extinct Plumas County city of Nevis. Deus was a laborer for the Red River Lumber Company who, just months earlier, had registered himself in Tuolumne County for the nation's second draft cycle. On December 6, 1917, however, Deus was found hanging from a pine tree near the Lake Almanor Dam. In his shirt pocket, a note was found reading, "I am a good German citizen."[192] There was little evidence to establish that Deus's death was a suicide, although the press seemed to think it was. Neither was it determined that the handwriting on the card belonged to him. No matter the circumstances of his death, Deus was ultimately the victim of the exhausting cross-pressures that accompanied living as a German American during the Great War.

Of those locals with the fortitude to speak up against the surge in xenophobia, the *Sacramento Bee*–owning McClatchy family possessed the highest profile. Perhaps it had something to do with the long, difficult road that Irish Catholics had endured against the nineteenth century's Nativists, Know-Nothings and the like. In any case, as early as July 1916, the *Bee* made it clear that its reporters were forbidden to "use the words 'Hun' or Huns' in news stories" and were instructed instead to use less-demeaning terms like "Teuton" or "Teutonic."[193] In July 1917, with America in full mobilization and school districts statewide dumping German instruction from their curricula, *Bee* owner and editor C.K. McClatchy wrote that he could "see no sense nor justice in extending the anger and even hate which American citizens righteously bear to Hohenzollerism, to the German people in general, who at heart are a noble, generous, thrifty, intelligent, enterprising and likable race. And certainly there is no scintilla of common sense in hating the German language."[194] And still, far from abiding dual loyalty, McClatchy called Columbia "a jealous mother" who demanded "from her sons and daughters—adopted as well as native—undivided allegiance."[195] It is also true—prior to the Great War and after—that the McClatchys, V.S. in particular, found plenty of reasons to be xenophobic when it came to the state's Japanese American population.

For all the effort expended by the APL, LL and others, not one of them ever caught a bona fide German spy.[196] Expressing one's affinity to an

Shown in 1909 is Sacramento's Turner Hall at 914 K Street, the Turnverein's meeting place until moving to 3349 J Street in 1925. *Sacramento Public Library.*

enemy nation, even a hostile rant against the president, military or Uncle Sam did not make one a spy, nor did it necessarily mean that one was an immediate security threat. But the impact of the Great War's vigilance groups resonated, even after the Armistice. Many of the valley's German Americans were forced to subvert their Germanness out of fear of where the tides of geopolitics might turn next and perhaps out of some measure of shame. Names became Anglicized—Welber changed to Waybur, Karl to Charles and the ennobling "von" was dropped from many surnames—and L Street's German Evangelical Lutheran Church, in the spring of 1918, suspended its German-language services because, in the words of Reverend Charles Oehler, "a man can have but one country…America is our country and we love it…let our people show what stuff they are made of."[197] By war's end, the same congregation also shed "German Evangelical" from its title, simply referring to itself as the St. John's Lutheran Church.

On November 12, 1918, just one day after the Armistice took effect, Frank J. Rumpf, in a simple comment charmingly accented with a few American idioms, spoke on behalf of Sacramento's ethnic German community by saying, "The

Americans of German descent here in Sacramento are mighty glad this thing is all over." For America's German demographic, the Great War represented a cultural tipping point whereby becoming more American was both essential and perhaps even unavoidable. Sacramento's Turnverein, a longtime cultural hub for the area's ethnic Germans, pushed on despite demands for its closure, as had been done with Joplin, Missouri's Turnverein, which liquidated itself and all its assets of $20,000 and then donated the sum to the American Red Cross. Sacramento's Turners vowed to stay around, but they also resolved to run all meetings in English, take notes in English and ensure that all classes—primarily gymnastics—and social events were conducted in English.

The loyalty hysteria of the Great War seemed to bleed seamlessly into the Red Scare of the 1920s. It was also common for former members of the now disbanded LL and APL to join forces with the newly formed and fully energized American Legion (AL), a group made up of former members of the American Expeditionary Force. The early AL's vision of Americanism—"100 percent Americanism," as stated in the group's preamble—meant a policy of zero tolerance toward foreign-affiliated labor organizations, the most jarring example of which came with a bloody standoff between the AL and IWW in Centralia, Washington, on Armistice Day 1919.

Closer to home, Sacramento's postwar May Days and Armistice Days stayed quiet, but the influence of the valley's AL affiliates grew. Joining forces with the longer-standing and like-minded Veterans of Foreign Wars (VFW) only bolstered the AL's sense of entitlement. The AL fought to remove what it considered to be un-American textbooks from the Marysville School District's history curriculum; it lobbied Sacramento's City Commission to "handle the IWW and Bolsheviki with a rigid hand" and "[give them] their just punishment"; and it gave Sacramento's General Services Department choice counsel on how to adequately display the American flag during holiday events.[198] It is also true that the AL looked to ease the unemployment pains of veterans by conducting, in concert with the State of California, American Legion Employment Day. Taking place every March 20, this day appealed "to the citizens of California to assist the American Legion to the fullest extent in providing a job for every ex-service man."[199] With the emergence of the Great Depression, however, nativist tendencies emerged, with both VFW and Legion officials seeking to affect public policy based on race and ethnicity. In 1930, the Sacramento AL lobbied California legislators to ban aliens from working on public works projects, while in 1932, Sacramento's local VFW chapter, Landsdale Post No. 67, actively urged local canneries to hire only white workers.[200]

Pictured in 1926 are members of Sacramento's VFW Post 67. Their interwar advocacy of veterans' issues could often stray into intolerance. *Sacramento Public Library*.

With the coming of the Second World War, and despite the growing power of the Legion and VFW, efforts to rehabilitate APL- and LL-like groups were repeatedly rejected by United States attorneys general Frank Murphy, Francis Biddle and Robert Jackson, all of whom were savvy to the ills of the Great War's vigilantism movement. This, however, provided the coldest of comfort in view of Japanese American internment, which came to serve as both a shameful reminder of America's ongoing inability to balance the protection of civil liberties with the demands of national security and, in the words of Progressive giant Hiram Johnson, an undying demonstration of how "war warps us, distorts our judgment, and destroys our sense of justice and our ideals."[201]

7

THE SEARCH FOR GREAT WAR MEMORY

By James C. Scott

The fanfare surrounding Sacramento's record-breaking Liberty Bond drives or the charm of a third-grader's war garden say a great deal about a community meeting its solemn national duty but little about the human cost of total war. Wrapped up in the roughly 450 Sacramento Valley residents who died in the Great War, and hardly accounted for in any final assessment, is the heartbreak suffered by mothers, wives, children and others who may have called them "friend." Valley soldiers fell under circumstances that should be considered quite heroic: dying while giving care to a comrade in the darkened trenches of Belleau Wood. In other cases, death came with little meaning at all: by way of a random virus, alone on a ship in the middle of the Atlantic Ocean. Essayist George Bernard Shaw referred to the enormity of death during the Great War, whether heroic or not, as "Godforsaken folly." Such personal tragedy became part of a largely suppressed subtext to the much more palatable promotion of the war via the popular press and the Committee on Public Information as a great reckoning between the democratic West and Prussianism.

A significant part of this chapter's intent will be to present the fullness of three valley lives cut short by the war. While all lived within the confines of Sacramento proper during a time when they quite possibly knew one another, each boy possessed his own unique origin and upbringing. The hope is that their stories are conveyed less in the vein of an obituary but more as a window into the simplicity and joy of Sacramento life as contrasted with the hardships that come with the ordeal of war.

Not one month after the Armistice, the Sacramento region set itself to capturing the memory of its Great War sacrifices through an assortment of means. These symbols of remembrance—some grown out of foreign seeds, some chiseled from granite and marble, some taking the form of grand parades on November 11—are part of what historian Susan-Mary Grant refers to as "the cult of the dead," a concept that emerged out of America's Civil War experience as a way of 1) educating morality and 2) cultivating the public's appreciation for sacrifice.[202] The significance of these expressions of memory has faded naturally, both through the attrition of time and by way of an obscurity brought on by the subsequent world war's weight and greater relevance to how we live today. And yet, their continued presence, not to mention the intent behind their creation, makes them intriguing and ultimately worthy of discussion.

Jennie Schuler had never been on an ocean liner before. As a Central Valley girl, born in Marysville and living the bulk of her life in Sacramento, the extent of her oceanic experience were trips to the Bay Area and the occasional sight of a wayward seagull. However, on this day—May 30, 1930—the sixty-five-year-old homemaker was quickly making up for lost time, peering from beneath the low brim of her newly purchased cloche hat down at the swirling waters of the Hudson River and New York Harbor. Her vantage point was the promenade of the ocean liner SS *America*, which in less than an hour would be yawing toward France and embarking on a journey that would bring Jennie as close to her son as she had been in twelve years.

Of the nearly 110,000 Americans who died in the Great War, 31,000 were never repatriated. As a simple matter of choice and War Department policy, next of kin could either have their sons sent back to America or interred overseas. To many, foreign burial not only seemed proper but also was the most profound expression of America's commitment to European peace. For those like President Theodore Roosevelt, whose own son Quentin died in the skies over France, it was more a matter of faith, quoting Ecclesiastes 11:3: "We have always believed, where the tree falls, there let it lie."[203]

And yet, with the 1920s churning on, both the pain of separation and lack of closure became too great a burden for many who had chosen to leave their loved ones overseas. As a result, Congress appropriated $5 million in 1929 so that those who desired to visit their sons or husbands could do so—at no cost and under better-than-average travel conditions. This group of roughly seven thousand women became known as the Gold

Star Pilgrims.[204] From Shasta County down to San Joaquin County, thirty-three Sacramento Valley women opted for pilgrimage. Seven, including Jennie Schuler, came from Sacramento County.

After the Armistice, it took nearly a decade for the roughly 2,400 known temporary burial locations of American servicemen throughout Belgium and France to be distilled into eight permanent cemeteries, all falling under the management of the American Battle Monuments Commission. Of that number, 6 sites—Meuse-Argonne, Aisne-Marne, Flanders Field, Somme, Oise-Aisne and Suresnes—would come to hold the bodies of twenty-one Sacramento County boys. Jennie's son Louis is buried at Aisne-Marne, a stunning forty-two-and-a-half-acre blend of white granite, finely coiffed grass and ancient farmland. It also sits at the foot of the elm-laden and legendary Belleau Wood, a spot where the modern U.S. Marines Corps came to grit out an epic name for itself.

While so many men grappled with the enlistment question, Louis Baptiste Schuler did not. Just two weeks after America's entry into the war, he volunteered for the U.S. Navy, enlisting on April 23, 1917. Prior to that, he had worked at Sixth and K's Kimball-Upson Sporting Goods store as a gunsmith, a job that provided a touch of irony for a young man who would eventually become a navy corpsman and saver of lives. He received his primary schooling at Mary J. Watson School at Sixteenth and J Streets, went on to graduate from Sacramento High School and spent much of his free time at the downtown YMCA while also worshiping at Saint Paul's Episcopal Church at Fifteenth and J. After mustering for service, Louis received his training at the Hospital Training School at Yerba Buena Island (known then as Goat Island), San Francisco, and then at the Marine Corps Hospital Training School in Quantico, Virginia. Exactly one year to the day after volunteering—April 23, 1918—he departed the Philadelphia Naval Shipyard, bound for France.

Once overseas, Louis went through the required stretch of in-country training. By June 21, he had been assigned to the Fifth Marine Regiment, a force that had been heavily engaged at the Chateau Thierry sector of Belleau Wood since June 1. Amid the confusion that came to characterize operations at Chateau Thierry is the lack of any true timeline of events beyond the fact that the marines attacked the opposing Prussian Guards in battalion-scale force on the same day Louis arrived. Again, with details so sparse, it is known only that, sometime during the evening—and on his first day of seeing combat—Louis was mortally wounded while doing his corpsman's duty. He held on for five more days, but on June 26, he was gone, having participated in what is considered to be the first large-scale operation for the Americans during the First World War.

Louis Baptiste Schuler in 1918. He was one of the first Sacramentans to volunteer after the Declaration of War. *California State Library.*

The average Sacramento Valley participant in the Great War would have likely worn the pine-tree patch of the Ninety-first Infantry Division and fought in the massive Meuse-Argonne Offensive of September–October 1918. In fact, most of the 130 Sacramento County men who died in the Great War fell at the Argonne Forest. One of those was Hugo Frank Wallner, an American-born ethnic German and son of master brewer Frank Wallner, a fixture at Frank Ruhstaller's City Brewery at Twelfth and H Streets. So much of Hugo's childhood in the Capital City seemed charmed. When not helping his father at the brewery—just a block west of the Wallner home at 1315 H Street—Hugo followed the standard path of German American acculturation by attending Sacramento schools, graduating from Sacramento High School in 1913 and worshiping at St. Francis of Assisi parish at Twenty-sixth and K Streets. He was also sociable, serving as one of nine who participated in an allegorical wedding that joined the west and east banks of the Yolo floodplain, helping celebrate the much-awaited opening of the Yolo Causeway in May 1916.

What seemed to truly distinguish Hugo from the rest of the crowd was his aptitude for mathematics, a subject he excelled at while in school and one that won him a job as a teller with the California National Bank. It also meant that Hugo was going a distinctly different direction from the rest of his siblings, who saw their futures in the brewing industry. Perhaps the highlight of his banking tenure was a February 1916 check-adding contest at the Travelers Hotel at Fifth and J. Sponsored by the American Institute of Banking. The so-called Burroughs Cup pitted thirty-six of the area's best tellers against one another in "an adding

Sacramento's Hugo Frank Wallner. The bank teller was the embodiment of German American assimilation. *California State Library.*

machine contest."[205] Hugo shined, accurately listing one hundred checks in a time of one minute, thirty-one seconds and beating the runner-up by four seconds.

Life found further meaning with an introduction to Miss Freda Caldarella, a bookkeeper with the Southern Pacific Railroad in Roseville. After a customary courting period, the couple was married on April 22, 1918. Just a few days later, Freda's picture appeared in the *Sacramento Bee*'s society section. Her profile revealed a sharp chin, soft eyes and a lush mane rolled into a bun, a style common for an American woman of this time soon entering into marriage.

Eight days later, courtesy of the nation's second round of draft call-ups, Hugo was off to Camp Lewis. It is far from surprising that the detail-minded bank teller was made clerk of Company B of the 361st Infantry Regiment. By late June, Hugo's unit had been transferred to France and what was to become the defining offensive of America's involvement in the Great War. Although occupying a position that would have ostensibly kept him well out of harm's way, he was made part of a unit that was tasked with the taking of Epinonville, which prior to the war had been a sleepy farming village, numbering some three hundred in population, but was now a key crossroads. As with Louis's case, specifics here are unclear. Hugo was injured on September 27. It was on that day that the 361st tried to take the village in three separate attempts, all of which were hurled back by a hail of machine gun and artillery fire. Hugo succumbed to his injuries on October 1.

Word of his death failed to make its way back to Sacramento until early November, a delay that was not uncommon for the time. With her husband away, Freda had been living with the Wallners in downtown Sacramento.

Beyond what must have been shock and heartbreak, it is impossible to know her next move. What we do know is that Freda eventually remarried, mothered a son and daughter and stayed in Northern California, passing away in San Francisco in 1983.

Like previous American wars, class divisions in civilian life came to loosely match those in the military. Officers, or those training to become officers, were typically upper- and upper-middle-class men who left college and business to become leaders. This was true of Mather's dauntless band of cadets and their quest for second lieutenant status, and it was certainly true of Gerald Loring Ebner of 1248 Thirty-ninth Street. Under the leadership of Gerald's German-born father, Frank, the Ebners amassed a large fortune, mainly through the wholesale wine business. Frank and his brother, Charles, were also the namesakes of the Ebner Hotel, originally known as the Ebner House, located at 116 K Street.

Of the family's six children, Gerald was the youngest. With his journey through the Sacramento public school system, he began to flower into an outstanding student and exceptional athlete. At Sacramento High School, the tall, brown-eyed, brown-haired Gerald starred on the football and track teams (880-yard dash), and by graduation in 1913, he had been given the prestigious "S" Award for his skill as a basketball player. He also enjoyed gymnastics as a member of the Sacramento Turnverein.

Sacramento High School's 1913 track team. Fourth from the left and wearing a black shirt is team captain Gerald Ebner. *Sacramento Public Library*.

Gerald's next destination was college at the University of California–Berkeley. It is there that he spent three years studying mechanical engineering, lettering in crew and experiencing Greek life as a member of Delta Kappa Epsilon. By the spring of 1916, he had earned both a college degree and a new name. From this point forward, Gerald insisted on being called "Jack." With his sharp new moniker in hand, he returned to Sacramento, spending the next year working for the Machine Shops of Skinner and Hansen at Fourteenth and U Streets. However, with the advent of war, Jack decided to join the army in October 1917.

He became one of the first cadets to attend Berkeley's ground school and eventually did his flight training at San Diego's North Island Naval Air Station. The soldier's life suited Jack. He quickly made an impression at North Island, where, as commander of his squadron, he won the reputation of being a "strict disciplinarian" and broke the school's point record on the machine gun range.[206] Jack was also the first in his class to fly solo and earned near-legendary status for landing his JN-4-D after the plane's engine died. Stellar throughout his time at North Island, Jack was commissioned as a second lieutenant on February 20, 1918, leaving North Island as the highest-scoring student in the school's short history.

Before heading to Hoboken, New Jersey, and transit to France, Jack came back to Sacramento to pay his family a final visit. Sitting in the Ebner home at 1248 Thirty-ninth Street, he expressed an eagerness to get overseas and, at last, experience real combat. What vexed him, however, was the thought of contracting pneumonia and never even making it to the fight. With that, Ebner headed east for transit on the ocean liner *Leviathan*, set to leave Hoboken on March 4. Just days prior to boarding, however, Jack came down with what appeared to be a simple cold. Not thinking much of it, he still made his way up the gangplank and onto the ship. Whatever ailed Jack progressed quickly. It was not until he was in the advanced stages of pneumonia that he informed the ship's doctor of his condition. He fought for a few days but succumbed to the infection on March 12.

Jack's death was tragic, but the way in which he died was far from rare. In fact, a bit more than half of America's Great War deaths came as a result of illness, many from the influenza pandemic of late 1918. It took Jack's mother, Josephine, until April 1 to learn of his death. Two weeks later, the Ebners—grasping to make Jack's death mean something—purchased a whopping $47,000 subscription in Sacramento's third Liberty Bond drive. Jack's body was repatriated, finally arriving in Sacramento on April 24.

After a brief memorial service at the family home, his body was interred at the family plot in Lot 86 of the Sacramento City Cemetery.

Before the Armistice was declared in November 1918, 128 more Sacramento County residents would die. With the war finally over, the question now was to what extent the capital region was willing to go to fossilize the memory of a war that so many Americans wanted nothing to do with—or so said a 1937 Gallup poll with 70 percent of its respondents believing that it had been a mistake for America to enter the war at all.[207] In actuality, the Sacramento region's support for Great War remembrance was strong, finding expression through a series of public and private projects.

The first came from the City of Sacramento. In December 1918, at the Native Sons' Hall at Eleventh and J Streets, mothers of the roughly 1,300 city men and women who had served in the Great War gathered together. Each was presented with a bronze medal showing an image of Sacramento City Hall wrapped inside a heart. At the top of the medal was a box that held a star for each child who served; 2 mothers had five stars, 6 had four, 42 had three, 227 had two and 1,028 had one. An inscription also read, "Presented by the City of Sacramento, Cal. Dec. 21st, 1918. To a Mother of Defenders of Liberty." With Governor William Stephens in attendance, Mayor Dan Carmichael told the group:

> *When we present you with this little token, we do so, realizing that during the years to come it may, in some degree tarnish and grow old, but with its age may we assure you will grow the thoughts of kindness, the thoughts of appreciation, the thoughts of love and esteem which we, the people of Sacramento, the donors of this badge, bear to you, to whom we give—the mothers of the defenders of liberty.*[208]

The medal presentation also included discussion about the immediate need for a "memorial hall in honor of Sacramento's brave soldiers."[209] This led to the construction of the Memorial Auditorium, which remains the Sacramento Region's single greatest commitment to remembering war dead. Construction of the $850,000 structure began in July 1925 and was finished in February 1927. The auditorium supplanted the Mary J. Watson Grammar School, the alma mater of Louis Baptiste Schuler, as a grand mix of Romanesque and Byzantine-style concepts that claimed an entire city block, between Fifteenth and Sixteenth and I and J Streets. To either side of the 3,500-seat venue's entrance are inscribed the words: "Dedicated to those who made the supreme sacrifice in the service of the United States." Six

Corinthian columns, each separated by seven Romanesque arches, highlight the building's impressive portico.

Other locations that were considered for the auditorium included the McKinley Park area and Tenth and I Streets. Financial backing for the project started in 1923, when Sacramento city residents approved a $750,000 bond issue. This added the auditorium to a long list of postwar Sacramento infrastructural and urban beautification projects that included two large city parks, an ultra-modern water filtration plant, two high-rise buildings on J Street, an incinerator and a new Southern Pacific train station, just to name a few.

Not long after the auditorium's opening, the city council voted to allow "local veterans organizations" to use it for one free night per year. This was typically designated for the annual Armistice Day Ball, put on by the Veterans of Foreign Wars, Lansdale Post No. 67. One of the more unique features of the auditorium were chimes that were procured in 1926 by the Sacramento chapter of the American War Mothers. At a cost of $11,000, they rang every fifteen minutes, while every evening at 6:00 p.m. they would

The Memorial Auditorium in 1927 at Fifteenth and J Streets. Just fifteen years earlier, Louis Baptiste Schuler was attending grammar school at the same spot. *Sacramento Public Library.*

chime "The Star-Spangled Banner." The chimes were silenced during the Second World War to help night shift workers sleep, resumed sounding in 1946, were removed in 1979 because of earthquake concerns and then were rehabilitated in 2005.

This idea of binding war memory to functional public structures also extended to state government. When the two capitol extension buildings were built in the late 1920s, the State Library and Courts wing included a

A 1950s image of the Memorial Auditorium's chimes, donated by the Sacramento War Mothers in 1926. Former mayor Bert Geisreiter looks on. *Center for Sacramento History.*

vestibule dedicated to Californians who fought in the First World War. Exquisite coffered ceilings were designed to give way to a mural of twelve images depicting warfare throughout the ages. The room's perimeter was also lined with imposing black columns, the marble for which was imported from the Italian island of Tino. At either end of the vestibule, Grecian-style urns were placed, resting below bronze inscriptions that on one end read, "This Vestibule Is a Memorial to the Men and Women Who Served the State and Nation During the World War" and on the other, "This House of Peace Shall Stand While Men Fear Not to Die in Its Defense."

Not only did Sacramento's William Land Park emerge in the early 1920s as an emerald oasis for recreation and diversion, but it also became a popular location for Great War remembrance, starting with a simple monument situated on Freeport Boulevard, between Thirteenth Avenue and Sutterville Road. Known throughout time as the "Eagle Monument," it was dedicated on Armistice Day 1926 by the Sacramento Women's Council in homage to Sacramento County's war dead. An eight-foot-high granite pyre accents the $2,000 structure, at the top of which sits a nest under the protection of a bronzed eagle, a symbol of the military safeguarding a nation at war. Listed on a bronze plaque are 119 of the 131 men and women from the Sacramento County who died in the Great War.

Farther west, and deeper into the park, more attempts were made to remember war dead. In May 1927, Sacramento's Lansdale Chapter of the Veterans for Foreign Wars (VFW) and the City of Sacramento agreed on an especially clever "living" memorial in Land Park. Members of the VFW brought home a number of seeds of trees native to the battlefields of northern France and Belgium. After incubating the seeds in the city nursery for a few years, they would then be planted along a primary stretch of road running through the center of the park, from Riverside Boulevard to Freeport Boulevard. Each tree—larch, maple, elm, hornbeam and others—would have a brass plaque bearing the name of a fallen soldier from Sacramento County. The road also would be renamed Memorial Drive. The last indication that anything had ever been done to see this through was a March 9, 1930 ceremony for the planting of the first sapling. A brief history of the tree—a beechnut and one of a planned total of 309—was given by Robert Protzman, post commander and the first Sacramento County man to pass his physical examination and qualify for service in the Great War. Mayor C.H.S. Bidwell then turned the sod. Beyond this point, however, the fate of the trees is unknown, and it is somewhat clear that "Memorial Drive" never stuck.

William Land Park's Eagle Memorial on Armistice Day 1926 and prior to Freeport Boulevard's expansion to four lanes in late 1957. *Sacramento Public Library.*

Memorial groves were a natural fit for a city so determined to become a city of trees and a park still filling out in flora. Land Park possesses two such spots. The American War Mothers dedicated the first in 1929. It sits just off Eleventh Avenue, between Riverside Boulevard and Thirteenth Street. A combination of coniferous and deciduous trees, the grove surrounds a small American flag and granite-mounted plaque that reads, "Sacramento Chapter, American War Mothers, Honor Grove, 1929. The trees in this grove were planted and dedicated to the mothers of this organization and to their sons and daughters who served in the World War." The other grove is situated at the intersection of Park Road and Fourteenth Avenue. Under the auspices of the Capital City Women, Post Number 389, it was dedicated on May 30, 1939, to all Sacramento women who served in the First World War.

Seven miles to the south of Land Park is what remains of Freeport Boulevard's "Victory Elms." Shrouded in a bit of mystery, the elms—planted to honor America's war dead and showcase the development of

Pictured is Land Park's memorial grove. Planted by Sacramento's chapter of the American War Mothers, it is located off Eleventh Avenue. *Sacramento Public Library.*

Freeport's Victory Elms line the west side of Highway 160. Some believe they were grown from seeds brought over from European battlefields. *Sacramento Public Library.*

the nation's transcontinental Victory Highway—are said to have grown out of seeds brought over from the battlefields of Europe by local doughboys. Yet no one knows when the planting occurred or what organizations were involved. Those who remember the elms in their prime speak of the cool shade that the tunnel-like canopy provided in the summer and the calming effect they offered throughout the year. First situated on both sides of the boulevard extending from the north of Freeport and then running through the town and to the south, most of the elms fell prey to the Dutch elm disease infestation of the late twentieth century. As of 2016, one can still grab an impressive glimpse of "what was" as a few hundred yards' worth of the elms still line the Boulevard just south of the Bartley Cavanagh golf course. Overtures to rehabilitate the elms have been sporadic at best, ensnared not in funding but in coding considerations and cooperation between both public and private entities.

In terms of physical spots for Great War remembrance, there remains little more in Sacramento County than what has been mentioned. Sometime in the late 1940s, the city christened a newly laid stretch of road in South Sacramento with the name Belleau Wood Lane, while in 1998 an obelisk was dedicated in Capitol Park as a remembrance to all Californians who gave their lives in service of the nation. Although lacking the permanence of granite or marble, Armistice Day parades facilitated by local VFW and AL posts were commonplace during the middle third of the twentieth century. Drum corps, grand marshals, Buddy poppies, marching bands and units from Mather and McClellan Air Force bases were frequent sights, moving along J and K Streets. One observance worthy of mention came during Sacramento's 1950 Armistice Day parade, when local Gold Star Mother and American War Mother chapters were guests of honor. The event started at 10:30 a.m. but was halted at 11:00 a.m. for a full minute of silence to honor those who gave their lives during the Great War. At the end of the pause, whistles from the Southern Pacific Shops were sounded and the parade resumed.

Perhaps one of the more unique Great War remembrances came in 1920, when Retta Parrott, a reference librarian for the Sacramento City Free Library, published a series of poems inspired by what she saw while looking out the windows of a newish Main Library at Eighth and I Streets. On April 19, 1919, she wrote "Winged Seeds," a dedication to what she perceived to be a city in spring-like transition from the concerns of war to those of peaceful renewal:

Of late the air is full of flying things:
Home making linnets, busy with romance,
New-risen butterflies that flit and glance,
And downy elm seeds trying out their wings;
Quite frequently is heard the whirr that brings
The airplane near, and searching the expanse
From side to side, we note the swift advance
Of man-made bird which through the ether sings:
The task of these has been to practice war
From the adjacent camp of Mather Field;
But now, most happily, war measures yield
To arts of peace, and monster planes fly o'er
The land, depositing their human freight
And friendly letters; seeds of love for hate.[210]

Little remains of the city that Louis, Hugo and Jack knew so well. Their downtown and East Sacramento homes are gone now, prey to old age, an ever-growing state government and the ongoing tide of urban infill. Their alma mater, Sacramento High School, then located at Nineteenth and L

Streets, was razed soon after the war, with the block it sat on now home to freshly built town houses and an array of chic bistros, confectionaries and bakeries. Joyland, the Pacific Gas and Electric streetcar line, Fairyland, the Riverside Baths, the Pantages Theatre and the Federal Building and Post Office at Seventh and K were all spots that they would have known well and frequented but now live in the city's collective memory as quaint curiosities of the past. What still exist are the mustering points for conscription districts one and two: city hall at Ninth and I and the California Fruit Building at Fourth and J, respectively. The Travelers Hotel, the spot of Hugo's banking glory, also stands, as do the St. Paul Episcopal Church at Fifteenth and J and the Saint Francis of Assisi Catholic Church at Twenty-sixth and K, where Louis and Hugo worshipped, respectively.

Visiting the spots where Hugo and Jack are buried is still quite possible. Jack's remains are somewhere within the Ebner family's fifteen- by fifteen-foot plot at the Old City Cemetery at Tenth and Broadway. The effects of time have left it far less polished than it would have looked in 1918. A single weathered obelisk tilts in the center of the plot, surrounded by patches of browning flora. As for Hugo, he is tucked away in the quiet and cool of a mausoleum basement at St. Mary's Catholic Cemetery in East Sacramento. Most of Sacramento proper's repatriated Great War dead are apportioned among these first two spots, along with East Lawn, St. Joseph's Catholic Cemetery and a few others.

It is not the fault of any one person or agency that the First World War remains such a forlorn chapter in American and Sacramento Valley history, nor is it too much of a challenge to understand why this is so. With the exception of two conflicts—the Civil War and the Second World War—every American war, including the First World War, can be soundly placed within the nation's basket of "forgotten wars." America's tenure in World War I was a short one. Of the eighteen months of involvement, the American Expeditionary Force (AEF) really was engaged in only three months of combat, with many historians arguing that although American entry into the war may have hastened its end, AEF involvement was far from decisive. France, England, Italy and all their colonial dependents had already done the heavy lifting. The Great War was truly a European struggle, reflected in a twenty-year postwar stretch that included an array of disillusioned poets, writers and artists (Siegfried Sassoon, Christopher Nevinson, David Jones and Erich Maria Remarque, to name just a few); major upheaval in social/caste structure; and likely, by way of an aversion to a future resembling anything close to trench warfare, barbed wire and chlorine gas, a move toward a more incremental approach to foreign policy, as evidenced by Great Britain and France's appeasement of Nazi imperialism during the 1930s.

There is also the notion that the Second World War became a much more self-defining war for America, with the nation's involvement being twice as long and contributions in both industry and war-making being indisputably decisive in ensuring an overall Allied victory. As historian John Milton Cooper Jr. states, "World War I was never the 'great war' for Americans the way it was for Britons and Europeans. It did not exert the same hold on American memory."[211] The hold that World War II has on the "American memory" also spawned from the conflict's many Yankee glories—a huge modernized army, hegemony in the Pacific and enormous economic leverage in Europe and Asia—which, in effect, made the second half of the twentieth century an undeniably American one.

In the end, what is left in modern American culture is a potpourri of Great War allusions: Snoopy chasing the Red Baron about the dangerous skies of northern France in his Sopwith Camel, Uncle Sam telling YOU to buy everything from football tickets to deodorant and the Sunday matinee showing Gary Cooper as *Sergeant York* winning the war with a series of homespun Tennessee turkey "whoops!" It hardly seems fair that the sincere efforts and sacrifices of so many so long ago should take a back seat to the strange ways of popular culture, yet for now they have. Perhaps the war's centennial changes that.

CONCLUSION

By Amanda G. DeWilde

Sacramentans celebrated the Armistice on November 11, 1918, with spontaneous abandon. Work ceased as thousands took to the streets in raucous revelry beginning in the early hours of the morning. They made noise any way they could, with empty cans, car horns and yelling building to a din. An elderly woman in Red Cross regalia wandered through the crowds waving her arms and dragging an empty oil can by a rope, while one man beat a steel tub with a four-foot piece of wood.[212] Formal celebration was far more restrained, with the city hosting a somber thanksgiving program at City Plaza on November 13 at the request of Mayor D.W. Carmichael. The service included band music, community singing, addresses by Governor William D. Stephens and Adjunct General J.J. Boree and prayers by Bishop W.H. Moreland and the Reverend S. Fraser Langford. In Marysville, citizens danced for half an hour in celebration of "the downfall of Hohenzollernism," the end of the German monarchy. But they danced under the supervision of a policeman and were required to don influenza masks throughout the evening.

The Spanish influenza epidemic that broke out in Sacramento in late October 1918 put a damper on many peace celebrations, as public gatherings were largely prohibited and ordinances required the wearing of gauze face masks. Brought to Sacramento by two children from Dunsmuir, the influenza epidemic spread quickly throughout the area and crested in late December 1918. When Sacramentans ventured outside on November 11 to celebrate peace, policemen decided against enforcing the mask law, and seventy-six additional cases of influenza were reported within two days.[213]

Crowds along K Street greet Belgian soldiers in parade celebrating the end of the world war. *Center for Sacramento History*.

About one in fourteen Sacramentans contracted the disease, and 10 percent of the cases were fatal, amounting to five hundred deaths over the course of just a few months. While the influenza epidemic tapered off, Germany negotiated the terms of its surrender with Allied countries for months after the Armistice, culminating in the signing of the Treaty of Versailles on June 28, 1919. This time, Sacramento celebrated the signing of the peace treaty with a last-minute mask-free gathering at the state capitol grounds, which included community singing and time for "celebration…of a spontaneous character."[214]

Fundraising for relief efforts kicked in immediately after the Armistice was announced. Sacramento's eight-day United War Work campaign to raise money for relief organizations began on November 11, but the effort faced the challenges of influenza and what the *Sacramento Bee* identified as "ribald anti-Americanism" in those who were not interested in donating to the cause.[215] Sacramento set for itself a quota of $250,000. While the Victory Boys and Victory Girls groups from local schools oversubscribed, Sacramento was exhausted and failed to meet its quota, falling short of the $250,000 goal by $75,000. The United War Work brigade was unable to overcome the dual foes of "General Apathy and General Indifference,"

Uncle Sam lifts his hammer toward $10,000,000 in Liberty Bond subscriptions above the post office on K Street. *California State Library.*

according to Chairman Charles E. Virden, who blamed the influenza epidemic.[216] From November 11 to 18, $104,800 went to Armenian and Syrian relief, fatherless children of France, local relief work, Belgian relief work and Jewish relief work. In addition, the Jewish Welfare Board, YMCA war work, Knights of Columbus, YWCA war work, the American Library Association, Salvation Army war work and War Camp Community Service received $145,200.[217]

Although the numbers didn't approach the toll of the Spanish influenza epidemic, the First World War took many of Sacramento's young men. Many also returned home with acute trauma, both physical and psychological.

At Letterman Hospital in San Francisco, Sacramento veterans received treatment for amputations, "mental derangements" and venereal disease. There, reconstruction aides also provided occupational therapy and educational service, helping soldiers "gain confidence and lose the highly-detrimental self-consciousness of the man maimed."[218]

Those who returned home safely were served by fledgling veterans' assistance programs. California provided for the rehabilitation of those disabled in service, including treatment, education and job placement. Governor William D. Stephens approached the State Council of Defense on November 2, 1918, with a proposal for a "comprehensive after-the-war program." The focus was on creating and finding jobs for returning soldiers, and he suggested a number of large-scale construction projects for them working in agriculture, horticulture and hydro-electric energy. He also urged an increase in the minimum wage that would "ensure the maintenance of the American standard of living." Stephens, who made veteran assistance and immigration key components of his policy, was reelected in November 1918 by a wide margin. He would serve as governor for five more years.

The future operation of Mather Field, the premiere flying school for army pilots, was uncertain at the end of the war. Mather Field was rapidly demobilized. Existing students were sent on to other posts to complete their training, and the flight school was officially closed in November 1919. Many returning soldiers from the Sacramento area took advantage of the city's new educational offerings and found work in the community. Hiram Albert, the draftee who trained at Fort Lewis, Washington, and whom we remember from an earlier chapter serving as an artillery man in the Ninety-first Infantry Division and then in the Meuse-Argonne Offensive of late 1918, returned home from France in 1919. After studying for a short time at the new Sacramento Junior College, he spent the next five decades working as an automobile mechanic with Sacramento's Universal Motor Company on 1520 K Street, the North Sacramento Garage on 1620 Del Paso Boulevard and Sacramento's Ford Motor Company at 1908 M Street. The last ten years of his work life were spent as a custodian at Sacramento High School.

A unique piece of legislation intended to reintegrate veterans by providing housing and work was the soldiers' Land Settlement Act.[219] A number of western states passed legislation giving preference to returning soldiers in applying for plots of land to settle and offering them loans to offset costs. In the Sacramento Valley, the experimental Durham Land Colony, 6,300 subdivided acres located near Chico, was to be their home. The colony had already been established by the California State Land Settlement Board to perfect land development methods. But within a couple years of the act's passage, all such experimental colonies in California were foundering. By 1925, a state legislative committee investigating the work in a similar settlement in Delhi, California, advised that "the State of California should never enter into another land settlement scheme."[220]

In addition to new postwar legislation addressing the needs of those returning from combat, laws that were passed as wartime measures found permanence after the war. The Wartime Prohibition Act was passed just after the war ended on November 18, 1918, and took effect at midnight on June 30, 1919, six months after the ratification of the Eighteenth Amendment prohibiting the production, sale and transport of intoxicating liquors. With the October 28, 1919 passage of the Volstead Act, which further defined and allowed enforcement of the Eighteenth Amendment, Sacramento entered the era of Prohibition. The Espionage and Sedition Acts passed during the war were also adjusted to a postwar reality. Although the Sedition Act amendments that prohibited disloyal speech about the United States government were repealed on March 3, 1921, the Espionage Act was ruled constitutional in 1919 and found to not be in violation of the First Amendment right to free speech. The core Espionage Act of 1917 remains in force as of 2015.

In interwar Sacramento, nativist groups and anti-foreign sentiment that first took root during the world war began to flourish. At a major Ku Klux Klan initiation on Lower Stockton Road in May 1922, four thousand were found in attendance. With the United States was no longer an ally of Japan, as it had been during the war, Sacramento strengthened its anti-Alien Land Law, and some sought to close state borders entirely to Japanese immigration, rescinding citizenship granted to the native-born by the Fourteenth Amendment. *Sacramento Bee* publisher V.S. McClatchy and Senator James D. Phelan partnered in efforts to prevent Japanese immigration, writing in 1921, "It is useless to attempt the making of good American citizens out of Japanese material."[221]

Throughout the war years, the power of labor unions increased. Now, the American Federation of Labor and local union organizers pushed for an eight-hour workday and the denial of shipping facilities to goods manufactured by children younger than sixteen through the establishment of an International Child Labor Law.[222] In an effort to protect their interests after the war, a number of agricultural associations had formed toward the tail end of the war, including the Grain Growers Association California, the Egyptian Cotton Growers' Association and the Central California Bean

Growers' Association. Also on the labor front, the Sacramento Business Women's Club fought for more equitable treatment in the workplace. When Miss Gail Laughlin, a San Francisco attorney, visited the club in November 1919, she argued against the federal government's assertion that "the women [were] satisfied with a sense of duty well done" despite unequal pay for Army Signal Corps women who served under shell fire but weren't granted military ranking or bonuses.[223] In the spring of 1919, telephone operators for the Pacific Telegraph and Telephone Company in Sacramento, all women, formed a union and struck for better pay. Women's rights groups, including suffragists, used the momentum of the war to persuade lawmakers to pass legislation like the Nineteenth Amendment, which gave women the right to vote at the national level on August 20, 1920.

Although the city, like many others, entered the war with some ambivalence, support had reached fever pitch by November 1918. Once the city recovered from the flu epidemic, Sacramento directed most of its energies and resources inward. At the end of the war, major employers were Liberty Iron Works, with around 1,500 men; the Southern Pacific and Western Pacific shops, employing 4,000; and several thousand more employed at the canneries. During the initial interwar years, referred to by E.M. Forster as "the long weekend," Sacramento enjoyed relief from the sacrifices of war and poured investment into building projects. New buildings that went up during the construction boom of the 1920s included the California Western State Life Insurance Building, Memorial Auditorium, the Elks Building, the Senator Hotel, the Berry Hotel, the California State Library and Office Building 1 and a new Southern Pacific passenger station. The California State Fairgrounds added the expansive Agriculture and Horticultural Building (later the Counties Exhibit Building). New communities formed associations as their populations expanded, reflecting the continuing diversity of Sacramento. Out of a growing South Asian population among migrant workers, Punjabi Muslims formed the Moslem Association of America in Sacramento in 1919, and the Hindu American Conference was founded in 1920.

Those returning from service abroad used their experiences to invest in the city. Anastasia Miller, the Red Cross nurse who served on the front lines in France during the last year of the war, established herself in the Sacramento medical community as founder and head of the Sacramento Red Cross Well Baby Clinic. The Red Cross had on hand about $70,000 left over from the war effort and decided to use the fund for local community needs rather than sending it to the national treasury. Started in May 1921, the Mothers' Education Center (later the Well Baby Clinic) offered free or reduced services to Sacramento mothers. The clinic would help to reduce infant mortality from its previously high figure of eighty-five per one thousand births. In addition to her work starting up the Well Baby Clinic, Miller was called "instrumental in obtaining equal rights for women war veterans." She was honored by the wives of Elks Club members as the first recipient of the Outstanding Woman of the Community award in 1947 and was named Woman of the Year by the Sacramento Soroptimist Club in 1952.

A year after the war ended, Sacramento celebrated its first Armistice Day with a parade. Among the celebrants marched veterans of the Spanish-American War and Border War against Pancho Villa, followed by "The Boys of '61"—veterans of the Civil War from both the Union and Confederacy. Great War veterans marched, too, with a little more diversity—women yeomen marched in their own contingent; Australian and Canadian veterans visited from the State Farm in Davis, where they were taking a course in farming; and autos carried recovering veterans from Letterman Hospital in San Francisco.[224] California Supreme Court justice Curtis D. Wilbur

Actors re-create a World War I–era tableau on a Veterans of Foreign Wars Post 67 parade float, 1938. *Sacramento Public Library*.

delivered an address at the capitol, celebrating the nation's "moral victory" and calling on Sacramento's young veterans to "marry and settle down, to give the Nation sons and daughters to maintain it, and to not complain that foreigners are bearing all the children."[225]

In November 1920, William D. Stephens declared Armistice Day a legal state holiday at the appeal of the American Legion. Its purpose was to pay tribute to the young men who gave their lives in the conflict, celebrate the preservation of American civilization and acknowledge the significance of Allied victory. The U.S. Congress recognized November 11 in 1926 with a resolution for a commemoration "designed to perpetuate peace through good will and mutual understanding between nations"; a congressional act in 1938 made Armistice Day (Veterans Day after 1954) a national holiday.

Seventy years after the Armistice, with the war a more distant memory, Sacramento held a special Veterans Day event at the Vietnam Memorial at Capitol Park to honor its oldest veterans. Traveling from the Veterans Home of California in Yountville and throughout the Sacramento area, fourteen World War I veterans in their nineties arrived to celebrate the seventy-first anniversary of the Armistice and share their stories.[226] By then, fewer than thirty people belonged to Sacramento's Barracks No. 216, Veterans of World War I, which met once a month in a veteran's hall on Stockton Boulevard. From Sacramento, Frieda Hardin, David Rowland, Stanley P. Klevan, Albert Guy Briggs, Max R. Isenberger, John Cucciere and Louis W. Palmer attended the ceremony. David Rowland, ninety-two, spoke at the event. He called for peace and shared John McCrae's World War I poem, "In Flanders Fields," which concludes, "To you from failing hands we throw the torch; be yours to hold it high. If ye break faith with us who die, we shall not sleep, though poppies grow in Flanders fields." Frieda Hardin, who served as a yeoman with the U.S. Navy from 1918 to 1920, placed a wreath at the foot of the Vietnam Memorial. She would be a featured speaker at the 1997 ceremony at Arlington National Cemetery at the age of one hundred. In the intervening years, we have lost the remaining veterans of the First World War, along with most of those who were old enough to remember life on the homefront during the war. But the legacy of service developed during the Great War, both on the homefront and abroad, lives on in Sacramento, "the Heart of California."

NOTES

Introduction

1. Henry Meade Bland, "The Great Orations of the Exposition," *Overland Monthly*, July–December 1915, 526.
2. *Sacramento Valley Monthly*, "Colonel Roosevelt Praises Sacramento Valley Display," August–September 1915, 22.
3. J.A. Filcher, *Official Report, Sacramento Valley Expositions Commission*, March 6, 1916, 43.
4. Ibid., 43.
5. Munro Smith, "America and the World War," *North American Review* 205, no. 738 (May 1917): 684.
6. Joseph A. McGowan, *History of the Sacramento Valley* (New York: Lewis Historical Publishing Co., 1961), 216.
7. Curt McConnell, *A Reliable Car and a Woman Who Knows It: The First Coast-to-Coast Auto Trips by Women, 1899–1916* (Jefferson, NC: McFarland & Co., 2000), 132–34.
8. "Unemployment in Certain Cities in the United States," *Monthly Review of the U.S. Bureau of Labor Statistics* 1, no. 5 (1915): 5–7.
9. "Sacramento's Greatest Building Year," in *Sacramento County in the Heart of California* (Chicago: American Library Association, 1917).
10. *Sacramento Bee*, "California Letters Flood Congressmen," April 7, 1917.

CHAPTER 1

11. *Sacramento Bee*, "Freedom Soldiers Leave 'Mid Cheers and Tears," September 5, 1917.
12. Ibid., "Patriotic Flame Is Fanned by Big Theater Gathering," April 11, 1917.
13. Warren S. Tryon, "The Draft in World War I," *Current History* 54, no. 322 (1968): 339.
14. Ibid., 340.
15. *Sacramento Bee*, "War Declaration Boosts Recruiting," April 6, 1917.
16. David M. Kennedy, *Over Here: The First World War and American Society* (Oxford, UK: Oxford University Press, 1980), 150.
17. State of California, *Statutes of California and Amendments to the Codes* (Sacramento, CA: Office of State Publishing, 1913), 649.
18. *Sacramento Bee*, "Not Even for Governor, Says Registrar, Refusing to Give Stephens Total," June 6, 1917.
19. *Sacramento Star*, "Registration Flashes," June 5, 1917.
20. *Sacramento Bee*, "Married Men Must Go; Claims Are Not Allowed," August 17, 1917.
21. Ibid., "Boasting Lodi Draft Resister Lands in Jail," September 20, 1917.
22. Ibid., "Home Ruler Is Defiant; Goes to Army," 15, 1917.
23. John Whiteclay Chambers, *To Raise an Army: The Draft Comes to Modern America* (New York: Free Press, 1987), 214.
24. *Sacramento Bee*, "Freedom Soldiers Leave."
25. Ibid., "Attorneys to Protect Interest of Drafted Men," July 29, 1917.
26. J. Roy Jones, *Memories, Men and Medicine: A History of Medicine in Sacramento* (Sacramento, CA: Sacramento Society for Medical Improvement, 1950), 195.
27. *Sacramento Bee*, "Marysville Man Is Supply Sergeant," February 2, 1918.
28. Ibid., "Men Spend Night in Realistic Trench Warfare," February 1918.
29. Ibid., "Kearny Soldiers Keep Many Dentists Rushing," August 7, 1918.
30. Ibid., "Camp Kearny Observes Day with Exercises," April 5, 1918.
31. Ibid., "Marysville Man Is Supply Sergeant," February 2, 1918.
32. Ibid., "Strong Requests End of Dance Halls," February 18, 1918.
33. Ibid., "Camp Lewis May Grow Vegetables," February 15, 1918.
34. 91st Division Publication Committee, *The Story of the 91st Division*, (San Mateo, CA: 91st Division Publication Committee, 1919), 23.
35. Jeanette Keith, "The Politics of Southern Draft Resistance, 1917–1918: Class, Race, and Conscription in the Rural South," *Journal of American Responsibility* 87, no. 4 (2001): 1,336.

CHAPTER 2

36. *Sacramento Bee*, "Sacramento Chosen by Uncle Sam," February 20, 1918.
37. Myrtle Shaw Lord, *A Sacramento Saga: Fifty Years of Achievement—Chamber of Commerce* (Sacramento, CA: Chamber of Commerce, 1946), 337.
38. Ibid., 339.
39. James J. Hudson, *Hostile Skies: A Combat History of the American Air Service in World War I* (Syracuse, NY: Syracuse University Press, 1968), 2.
40. *Sacramento Bee*, "Sacramento Chosen by Uncle Sam."
41. Ibid., "Government May Demand Cleanup of Sacramento," April 8, 1918.
42. Ibid., "Sacramento Must Proceed to Clean Up," April 9, 1917.
43. *Wing Tips*, "Cadet Recalls Mather in Its Early Years," October 30, 1981.
44. Ibid.
45. Ibid.
46. *Sacramento Bee*, "Flights from Mather," September 12, 1918.
47. Alvin K. Matthews, "A Story of Pigeons," *Air Currents*, December 1918.
48. *Sacramento Bee*, "Flights from Mather."
49. Lord, *Sacramento Saga*, 342.
50. *Sacramento Star*, "Plans Here for U.S. Planes," October 10, 1917.
51. Ibid., "Pro-Germans Try to Start Trouble at Aeroplane Plant," December 2, 1917.
52. *Sacramento Bee*, "Airplane Plant Construction Is Now Under Way," October 5, 1917.
53. *Hearings before Subcommittee No. 1 (Aviation) of the Select Committee on Expenditures in the War Department, United States House of Representatives*, 66th Congress (1919). Testimony of J.M. Henderson Jr., Sacramento, CA.
54. Ibid.

CHAPTER 3

55. *Sacramento: The Heart of California* (Sacramento, CA: Chamber of Commerce, 1914), 1.
56. *Sacramento Union*, "Increased Production Aid in National Crisis," April 2, 1917.
57. *Sacramento Bee*, "Grow More Crops, Farmers Will Be Urged," April 3, 1917.
58. David Vaught, *Cultivating California: Growers, Specialty Crops, and Labor, 1875–1920*, (Baltimore, MD: Johns Hopkins University Press, 1999), 164.
59. *Sunday Leader*, "Experts Discuss County's Part in Food Crisis," April 22, 1917.
60. Ibid., "Food Crisis Keynote at University Farm Fete," April 29, 1917.
61. Thomas Forsyth Hunt, "War Emergency Farm Bureaus," *University of California Journal of Agriculture* 5, no. 1 (1917): 1.

62. *Sunday Leader*, "Fifty Agricultural Clubs to Be Formed," November 11, 1917.
63. *Folsom Telegraph*, "Over There," February 22, 1918.
64. *Sunday Leader*, "Big Crowds Attend State Fair Opening," September 1, 1918.
65. *Pacific Rural Press*, "Tractors for Orchard and Beans," July 6, 1918.
66. Ibid., "See the State Fair Tractor Tent," September 1, 1917.
67. *Pacific Rural Press*, "Truck Saves Time and Fruit," September 1, 1917.
68. *California Cultivator*, April 6, 1918, 445.
69. *Sacramento Bee*, "More Labor Is Demand of Farmers," May 12, 1917.
70. *Sunday Leader*, "Labor Scarcity Not Serious Is Lubin's Opinion," May 13, 1917.
71. Emil T.H. Bunje, *The Story of Japanese Farming in California* (Washington, D.C.: Works Progress Administration, 1971), 26.
72. *Galt Herald*, "Japanese Ask Change in Alien Land Law," September 6, 1918.
73. *Sunday Leader*, "Dire Labor Shortage on Farms Feared," April 28, 1918.
74. Catherine Gabriel Kipp, *Women on the Land, The Women's Land Army: California, Northern Division, 1918–1920* (MA thesis, Sacramento State University, 1960), 48.
75. *Pacific Rural Press*, "The Women's Land Army," June 8, 1918.
76. *Sacramento Bee*, June 15, 1918, 4.
77. *Sunday Leader*, "Women's Land Army to Pick Florin Grapes," August 25, 1918.
78. *Sacramento Bee*, "California Doing Her Bit to Help Food Situation," September 18, 1918; Sacramento Chamber of Commerce, Bureau of Service, *Sacramento, The Gateway to California*, (Sacramento, CA: The Bureau, 1922), 20, 21.
79. *Sacramento Bee*, "$400,000 War Order Comes to This City," August 26, 1917.
80. Ibid., "Sacramento Valley Grain Crop Breaks Records for Nearly Quarter Century," July 30, 1918.
81. *Caterpillar Times*, "Sacramento Establishes a Garden," February 1918, 12.
82. *Sunday Leader*, "Wheatless Day Is Coming on S.P. Cars and Cafes," October 21, 1917.
83. *Sacramento Bee*, "'Sweetless Day' but Partially Observed," November 15, 1917.
84. *Sunday Leader*, "'Showy Eating' to be Tabooed at Luncheon: Ask Women to Aid," November 4, 1917.
85. Ibid., "State Will Use War Bread in Napa Hospital," July 30, 1917.
86. Ibid., "After December 10th Bread Will Have a Different Flavor," November 25, 1917.
87. Ord. no. 322 3rd Sec., passed December 13, 1917; Sacramento, *Ordinances of the City of Sacramento* (Sacramento, CA: Independent Printing Co., 1924), 243.
88. *Sacramento Bee*, "Strict Food Rules for Restaurants Are Announced," October 13, 1918.

Chapter 4

89. *Sacramento Bee*, "Women of Sacramento March for Fourth Liberty Loan," October 10, 1918.
90. Mrs. Nevada Davis Hitchcock, "The Mobilization of Women," *Annals of the American Academy of Political and Social Science* 78 (July 1918): 25.
91. *Sunday Leader*, "Women Respond to Country's Call," June 24, 1917.
92. Ibid., "Patriotic Mass Meeting of All Women Is Called," July 8, 1917.
93. Orangevale Women's Club, *Orangevale Women's Club History, 1913–1973* (n.p., 1973), 1–2.
94. Sacramento Women's Council, *A Silhouette of Service* (Sacramento, CA: News Publishing Company, 1955), 27.
95. G. Walter Reed, *History of Sacramento County, California* (Los Angeles: Historic Record Co., 1923), 416.
96. *Sacramento Bee*, "Big Sum Is Secured for Red Cross," May 5, 1917.
97. *Sunday Leader*, "Red Cross War Fund Campaign Opened with Appealing Pageant," May 19, 1918.
98. *Sacramento Union*, "Soldiers Are Greeted by Local Women," August 13, 1918.
99. *Sacramento Bee*, "Trained Nurses Should Enroll: Girls Needed for Training," June 6, 1918.
100. Ibid., "27 Have Signed as Student Nurses," August 8, 1918.
101. *Sacramento Union*, "45 Sacramento Nurses in Service," October 6, 1918.
102. May 25, 1918 letter, Anastasia Miller Papers, MC 36, Sacramento Room, Sacramento Public Library, Sacramento, California.
103. December 1, 1918 letter, Anastasia Miller Papers, MC 36, Sacramento Room, Sacramento Public Library, Sacramento, California.
104. *Sunday Leader*, "Influenza Is on the Decrease Say Physicians," November 3, 1918.
105. *Sacramento Bee*, "57 Women Caring for City's Sick," November 12, 1918.
106. Lettie Gavin, *American Women in World War I: They Also Served* (Niwot: University Press of Colorado, 1997), 1.
107. *Sacramento Bee*, "Two Sacramento Girls, Yeomen in the Navy, Ordered to Washington," April 13, 1918.
108. *Kansas City Star*, "Given a Soldier's Burial," May 1, 1918.
109. *Sacramento Bee*, "Sacramento Nurse Tells of Farewell Services in New York," March 21, 1918.
110. Ibid., "Hospital Sorrows Told of by Nurse," September 19, 1918.
111. A.B. Wolfe and Helen Olson, "War-Time Industrial Employment of Women in the United States," *Journal of Political Economy* 27, no. 8 (October 1919): 667.
112. United States, Department of Labor, Bureau of Labor Statistics, "Women in Industry," *Monthly Labor Review* (November 1918): 184.

113. *Sacramento Union*, "Girl Savs [*sic*] 5 Cents Was 3 Days' Pay," August 2, 1918.
114. *Sunday Leader*, "Women Will Start Work Tomorrow in S.P. Shops," August 19, 1917.
115. Robert A. Pecotich, *Southern Pacific's Sacramento Shops: Incubator of Innovation* (Berkeley, CA: Signature Press, 2010), 312–13.
116. *Sacramento Union*, "Want Women to Learn Telegraphy," September 30, 1917.
117. Ibid., "Sacramento Has Auto Saleswoman," September 25, 1917; "Christie Pleased with Saleswoman," September 30, 1917.
118. *Sacramento Bee*, "Galt Woman Wins Justice of Peace Office; Says Women Aid Politics," November 9, 1918.
119. *Sunday Leader*, "Girl Winner of Tractor Prize Joins Women's Army," June 16, 1918.
120. *New York Times*, "Girl as Driver of Tractor," June 23, 1918.
121. Jessica B. Peixotto, "The Children's Year and the Women's Committee," *Annals of the American Academy of Political and Social Science* 79 (September 1918): 259.
122. *Sunday Leader*, "Local Woman Is Winner of Better Mothers' Contest," September 5, 1918.
123. Joseph Lee, "War Camp Community Service," *Annals of the American Academy of Political and Social Science* 79 (September 1918): 193.
124. *Sacramento Union*, "Looking after the Boys," August 4, 1918.
125. Sacramento Women's Council, *Silhouette*, 22.
126. *Sacramento Union*, "Women Jury Bill Passes Senate," April 3, 1917.
127. *Sacramento Bee*, "Federated Union Urges Women to Quit War Jobs," November 9, 1918.
128. Hitchcock, "Mobilization," 31.

CHAPTER 5

129. California, Governor (1917–1923: Stephens), California Historical Survey Commission, War History Department, *California in the War: Addresses Delivered at State War Council Held Under the Auspices of the State Council of Defense, San Francisco, March 5–6, 1918* (Sacramento: California State Printing Office, 1921), 7.
130. Sacramento High School, *The Review* (Sacramento, CA: Student Body of Sacramento High School, June 1910), 105.
131. *Sacramento Bee*, "School Authorities Asked to Prohibit German Songs," May 16, 1917.
132. California Board of Education, "Report of the Textbook Committee," *Third Biennial Report of the State Board of Education, 1916–1918* (Sacramento, CA: State Printing Office, 1918), 34.

133. *Sacramento Union*, "Hughes Objects to German Language in High Schools," August 17, 1918.
134. *Folsom Telegraph*, "To Form Debating League for Schools," August 28, 1918.
135. *Galt Herald*, "Parent-Teachers Urge Children to Purchase Thrift Stamps, February 1, 1918.
136. California Department of Public Instruction, *Twenty-ninth Biennial Report of the Superintendent of Public Instruction* (Sacramento: California State Printing Office, 1920), 20.
137. *Sunday Leader*, "Little Interest in Alien Schools, April 15, 1917.
138. California Department of Parks and Recreation, Office of Historic Preservation, *Five Views* (Sacramento, CA: State Printing Office, 1988), 196.
139. *Sacramento Union*, "Special Schools for Followers of Fruit," October 3, 1918.
140. California Commission of Immigration and Housing, *A Manual for Home Teachers* (Sacramento, CA: State Printing Office, 1918), 17.
141. Sacramento High School, *The Review* (June 1918): 49.
142. *Sunday Leader*, "Schools Asked to Aid in Attack on Food Wastage," December 16, 1917.
143. Sacramento High School, *The Review* (June 1917): 82–83.
144. Sacramento School Department, *Annual Report, 1917–18–19* (Sacramento, CA: School Department), 93.
145. *Sacramento Bee*, "Red Cross Work Favored by Girls," December 8, 1917.
146. *Folsom Telegraph*, "'Sister Susie's Sewing Socks for Suffering Soldiers,'" May 18, 1917.
147. *Sacramento Bee*, "Teachers Working with Victory Children," November 13, 1918.
148. Ibid., "10,000 Children Ready to Plead for War Funds," October 23, 1917.
149. Ibid., "Schools Hurry to Train Army of Telegraphers," December 8, 1917.
150. Sacramento High School, *The Review* (February 1921): 27.
151. Sacramento Women's Council, *A Silhouette of Service* (Sacramento, CA: News Publishing Company, 1955), 26.
152. *Sunday Leader*, "Turn Scores School Clubs," May 13, 1917.
153. *Sacramento Bee*, "Military Training Planned for High School Boys," January 24, 1918.
154. *Sunday Leader*, "Cadets Finish War Training at Del Paso Park," April 14, 1918.
155. *Sacramento Bee*, "Grass Valley High School Girls Take Military Drill," May 17, 1917.
156. *Sacramento Union*, "Ione School Boys Would Go to War," April 14, 1917.
157. John F. Lafferty, *The Preston School of Industry, A Centennial History* (Ione, CA: Preston School of Industry, 1994), 120–21.
158. *Folsom Transcript*, "Youth Urged to Remain in School," August 2, 1918.
159. *Sunday Leader*, "Students Engaged in Studies of Military Value Will Be Allowed to Continue in College," September 8, 1918.

160. Charles J. Falk, *The Development and Organization of Education in California* (New York: Harcourt, Brace & World, 1968), 46.
161. Jan Hang and Ann McHatton, eds., *Celebrating 90 Years: Sacramento City College, 1916–2006* (Sacramento, CA: Sacramento City College, 2006), 6.
162. *Sacramento Bee*, "Teacher Weds; Old Problem Bobs Up," August 17, 1917.
163. Ibid., "Educators Are in Favor of School Centralization," October 11, 1918.
164. "The Sacramento Teachers' War Service League," *Journal of Education* 88, no. 1 (July 1918): 20–21.
165. California Board of Education, *All for America: What California Schools Can Do in the Present Crisis* (Sacramento, CA: State Printing Office, 1917), 13.
166. *Sacramento Bee*, "League to Purge Schools of Disloyalty," January 25, 1918.
167. *Sacramento Union*, "Charges Made Against Teachers," September 25, 1917.
168. Ibid., "Education Board Decides Monday in Teacher Cases," November 11, 1917.
169. *Sacramento Union*, "Disloyal Teacher Barred from Schools," August 7, 1918.
170. *Lodi Sentinel*, "Revoke License of Myra Dunton," August 10, 1918.
171. Sacramento School Department, *Annual Report*, 9.

CHAPTER 6

172. *Sacramento Bee*, "School Boys Thrash Unpatriotic Comrade," April 9, 1917.
173. Daniel Farber, *Security v. Liberty: Conflicts Between National Security and Civil Liberties* (New York: Russell Sage Foundation, 2008), 31.
174. Frederick Luebke, *Bonds of Loyalty: German Americans and World War I* (DeKalb: Northern Illinois University Press, 1974), 65.
175. Amber Smith, "A Full Measure: The German-Americans in Tracy, California: 1917–1918," *Pacific Historian* 28, no. 1 (1984): 53.
176. *Sacramento Bee*, "Autoist Terrorized by Home Guard," September 1, 1917.
177. *Sacramento Star*, "Your Neighbor, Your Maid, Your Lawyer, Your Waiter," April 17, 1918.
178. *Sacramento Bee*, "Big Intelligence Body Is Planned," April 7, 1917, 12.
179. Kennedy, *Over Here*, 81.
180. Christopher Capozzola, *Uncle San Wants You: World War I and the Making of the Modern American Citizen* (Oxford, UK: Oxford University Press, 2012), 122.
181. *Sacramento Star*, "Judge Shields Leads Move to Stop Sedition," April 11, 1918.
182. Michael Sulick, *Spying in America* (Washington, D.C.: Georgetown University Press, 2012), 121.
183. Stephen Vaughn, *Holding Fast the Inner Lines: Democracy, Nationalism, and the Committee on Public Information* (Chapel Hill: University of North Carolina Press, 1980), 216.
184. Luebke, *Bonds of Loyalty*, 213.

185. David Frum, *How We Got Here: the 70's: The Decade That Brought You Modern Life (For Better or Worse)* (New York: Basic Books, 2000), 267.
186. *Sunday Leader*, "Merchant Is Quizzed by Liberty League," April 28, 1918.
187. *Sacramento Star*, "Liberty League Puts Hotel Man Under Hot Fire," April 27, 1918.
188. Ibid., "Sedition Cases Are Taken Up by U.S. Grand Jury," May 21, 1918.
189. Smith, "Full Measure," 60.
190. Ibid.
191. *Sacramento Bee*, "Forced to Kiss Flag and Leave Town," April 11, 1917.
192. Ibid., "'I'm a Good German,' Says Card on Dead German," December 7, 1917.
193. Steve Wiegand, *Papers of Permanence: The First 150 Years of the McClatchy Company* (Sacramento, CA: McClatchy Company, 2007), 117.
194. C.K. McClatchy, *Private Thinks By C.K.* (New York: Scribner, 1936), 153.
195. Ibid., 150.
196. Christopher Capozzola, "The Only Badge Needed Is Your Patriotic Fervor: Vigilance, Coercion, and the Law in World War I America," *Journal of American History* 88, no. 4 (2002): 1,360–61.
197. *Sacramento Star*, "Church to Stop German Service," April 30, 1918.
198. *Sacramento Bee*, "Ex-Service Men Request City Commission be Firm with Anarchists," November 25, 1919
199. Ibid., "Employment Day for Ex-Service Men," March 11, 1922.
200. Ibid., "War Veterans Seek Law Banning Aliens From Public Works," December 10, 1930; "Veterans Urge Use of Whites in Canneries Here," February 12, 1932.
201. Hiram Johnson, *The Diary Letters of Hiram Johnson, 1917–1945*, ed. Robert E. Burke (New York: Garland Publishing, 1983), 375.

Chapter 7

202. Susan-Mary Grant, "Raising the Dead: War, Memory and the American Identity," *Nations and Nationalism* 11, no. 4 (2005): 509.
203. Ralph E. Shannon and F.W. Graham, "Bring the War Dead Home," *Rotarian* 69, no. 5 (1946): 20
204. In May 1918, President Woodrow Wilson approved the idea that instead of wearing black clothing in the mourning of a dead son or daughter, American mothers should wear a black armband with a gold star representing every child lost in service to the nation. Service flags with gold stars were also approved.

205. *Sacramento Bee*, "Wallner Wins Cup in Adding Machine Contest," February 26, 1916.
206. "Pro Patria Mortui," *California Alumni Fortnightly* 11, no. 7 (1918): 169.
207. John Milton Cooper, "The Great War and American Memory," *Virginia Quarterly Review* 79, no. 1 (2003): 81.
208. *Sacramento Bee*, "$150,000 Memorial Hall Is Promised," December 23, 1918.
209. Ibid.
210. Retta Parrott, *Library Windows* (Sacramento, CA: Sacramento Public Library, 1922), 42.
211. Cooper, "Great War," 84.

Conclusion

212. *Sacramento Bee*, "Thousands Quit Work to Celebrate," November 11, 1918.
213. Ibid., "Carelessness in Celebrating Causes Increase," November 13, 1918.
214. Ibid., "Peace Celebration at Capitol Tonight," June 30, 1919.
215. Ibid., "War Work Campaigners Find Many Vocal Patriots in Town," November 14, 1918.
216. Ibid., "Sacramento Fails to Reach Goal in War Work Drive," November 21, 1918.
217. Ibid., "Division of War Work Fund Is Explained," November 15, 1918.
218. *The History of Letterman General Hospital* (San Francisco, CA: Listening Post, Presidio, 1919), 16.
219. California State Land Settlement Board, *Information Regarding Progress under the Land Settlement Act of the State of California and About the Plans of Soldier Settlement in the Future* (Sacramento: California State Printing Office, 1919), 5.
220. California Legislature, Joint Legislative Committee Investigating State Land Settlement at Delhi, Calif. Committee Report, *Assembly Journal* (1925): 937.
221. V.S. McClatchy, "Japanese in the Melting Pot: Can They Assimilate and Make Good Citizens?" *Annals of the American Academy of Political and Social Science* 93 (January 1921): 29.
222. *Sacramento Bee*, "Organized Labor Wants Universal Eight-Hour Day," November 15, 1918.
223. Ibid., "Speaker Says Women Founded Industries," November 12, 1919.
224. Ibid., "Heroes of War Pay Honor to Those Who Died," November 11, 1919.
225. Ibid., "Armistice Day Speaker Urges Men to Marry," November 11, 1918.
226. Ibid., "Veterans of 'War to End War' Honored," November 12, 1989.

INDEX

M

N

O

P

R

S

Y

ABOUT THE AUTHORS

Amanda G. DeWilde has served as the archivist for the Special Collections of the Sacramento Public Library since 2010, working in the Sacramento Room of the Central Library. DeWilde earned her bachelor's degree in history from Southern Oregon University and her master's degree in information studies with an emphasis in archival studies from the University of Texas–Austin. She and her husband reside in Folsom.

James C. Scott has been a reference librarian with the Sacramento Public Library since 2000. For most of that period, he has worked in SPL's Sacramento Room, where he has coauthored four other books on Sacramento history. He holds a bachelor's degree in history and political science from Marquette University and has master's degrees in European history and library and information science. He lives in East Sacramento with his wife, son and a black and tan dachshund called Schweinsteiger.

Set in the original 1917 Carnegie Foundation–funded section of the Sacramento Public Library, the Sacramento Room was founded in 1995 as an archives and special collections for primary and secondary research materials relative to the history of the Sacramento Region. Its rare book, book art, map, city directory, photograph, digital and manuscript collections make it one of the premier spots for historical research in Northern California. The Sacramento Room can be visited online at www.saclibrary.org/locations/sacramento-room.